...art of
Lynne O'Sullivan's life ever
since she had a story
published in *Bunty* magazine
when she was ten. She
currently juggles her creative
life around her day job as a
personal assistant. Her stories
and plays have received
public readings and she studies art in her minimal spare
time. Having trained as an actress, Lynne also appears
in plays on the London fringe.

LYNNE O'SULLIVAN

BACK ALONG THE TRACK

Matador
9 De Montfort Mews
Leicester LE1 7FW, UK
Tel: (+44) 116 255 9311 / 9312
Email: books@troubador.co.uk
Web: www.troubador.co.uk/matador

ISBN 978 1906510 671

A Cataloguing-in-Publication (CIP) catalogue record for this book
is available from the British Library.

Cover photograph by Ian Markham.

Typeset in 11pt Bembo by Troubador Publishing Ltd, Leicester, UK
Printed in the UK by Biddles Ltd, King's Lynn, Norfolk

Matador is an imprint of Troubador Publishing Ltd

For my father

Names have been changed for privacy, apart from those of my immediate family. All characters are remembered with respect.

Sunday Around My Father

I was born in Willesborough where I would wake on Sunday mornings to a single bell calling people to church. Back then in the late fifties, Willesborough was a sleepy suburb of Ashford, which had also started to wake from being a quaint little market town in the heart of Kent to the busy place that it is today. By the time I was nine years old in 1962, it was growing both in population and industry, the main one being the railway works which had first opened in the 1840s.

Throughout my childhood the sound of train wheels was always in the background. Passenger trains sped up to London from the coast and wagons shunted along the tracks in the railway factory where my father, like many of the town's men, was employed. On Sundays the trains went at a slower pace but, like Dad, they still worked. He would emerge from his bedroom stretching and yawning in pyjamas that had usually seen better days, but he was too preoccupied with what could be accomplished before sunset to care about his worn out paisleys. Mum would soon have them on the washing line billowing in the breeze with all the rest of the laundry from the kitchen floor and a dozen nappies belonging to our baby sister Anne.

Each weekday morning Dad would be up early to go to the railway. He hated being late and, on the rare occasions he was likely to miss the seven-thirty clocking-in deadline, would shout and stomp about, declaring that it was all Mum's fault as he hunted for his keys or the 'Doorstep' sandwich that he took for lunch. My brother Will and I knew to keep out of his way at such times and would hide ourselves beneath the coats hanging in the hall. If we were caught sniggering when Dad tripped over a toy or yanked on his boot only to have the lace break in his hand there would be hell to pay. Not that he ever hit us – his voice was enough. When Dad was safely out of the house, Will and I would watch from the little window on the stairs as he leapt into whatever car he had at the time and shoot off down the road like a bat out of hell. Once, this was a Mini in which he looked enormous, like Officer Dibble on 'Top Cat,' we decided.

Dad's usual work plan on Sundays was to graft down 'the yard'. This was not our back yard that a flimsy, glass panelled door with its S-shaped handle opened out to, but a plot of land a mile or two away in an old part of Willesborough called 'The Lees'. The yard was at the end of a lane leading off the main road, a stone's throw from the hospital where my sister Maureen (Mo) and I had been born within a two years of each other. There Dad would toil come rain or shine, breaking up old cars for scrap. It was hard, exhausting work from which he seldom spared himself unless he was really ill and then he'd have to be half dead before he would take any time off. He'd come home at the end of the day as black as coal, his hair full of axle grease but with a satisfied smile on his face.

Dad often said the yard had been bought with blood, sweat and tears. Sweat and tears was probably true as he had sweated and cried over all the work it took to buy the piece of land, but there had been no blood to speak of – that would come later. He'd purchased the yard from Tom, an elderly man in Newtown, with every penny he had saved. Nurturing the possibility of the sale, he had looked after the ailing gentleman for many months doing him every service from shopping to cutting his toenails. He and Tom ended up good friends, aside from their deal over the plot of land.

If we children turned up at the yard on a sunny afternoon with our mother, Dad would make us tea. He'd laugh when I turned up my nose as he rinsed the cups clean of dead flies and wasps.

'Whassup?' he'd say. ''Tis only wapses!'

The tea would be served in an old sun-blistered railway carriage where weeds grew up through the floor and nettles pushed in through the windows. I would imagine myself a fine lady passenger going up to London in a long dress. Will would be in his element, running about exploring the wrecks of old cars while Anne sat on the floor playing with couple of spanners.

When Dad first bought the yard, from which he intended to run a car breaking business, I had been off school with German measles and had helped him to tidy the place up. In my case, this meant moving a few bits of wood around and cutting the grass along the corrugated iron fence. Most of the time I messed about, climbing and picking fruit from the trees. At lunch time Dad and I would walk up to the dairy shop together for a pint of milk each and a pie.

Those few days back then before Will grew big enough to help with the work were the most that I had spent alone with Dad in my life. During this time we bonded in a rough sort of way, even though we didn't talk much. I would lie on the roof of that old railway carriage staring up the vast expanse of sky while Dad tinkered about, humming an old Irish ballad or something by Jim Reeves.

Sometimes I would take Dad's dog, an Alsatian called 'General', for a run in the Broomfields. This was a wooded area that stretched from Willesborough to Hinxhill. Both the dog and I were young then and we'd bound along together, leaping effortlessly over grass and nettles with the hedgerows waving behind us. There wasn't much point in putting General on a lead as, if he decided to bolt, I couldn't have stopped him. He was delighted to be free from the confines of the yard and the old Zephyr that was his bed. When Dad brought him to the house once it was terrifying, like having a wolf rampaging through the rooms. General was so excited at seeing us all that he couldn't help jumping up. The weight of his paws alone was enough to knock us to the ground.

In winter, the yard was a desolate place to be. On the darkest afternoon when most people were curled up in front of their fires, Dad could be found down there prizing off old tyres, curses steaming out of his mouth with only General for company.

Dad was proud of his piece of land but it didn't really mean much to us children as, of course, we lived only for the present. On Sundays I would be off to 'The Tree' after breakfast with my friend Patty. 'The Tree' was a little glade near the churchyard where, like tomboys, we'd play at making bows and arrows, swing from branches or climb 'Herbert', a tall, leafless tree which had once been struck by lightening. Will would always be out playing with Mick from over the fence.

'My Jaysis, ye has it grand, ye lot,' Dad would laugh. He was forever comparing what he considered to be our 'privileged' childhood with that of his own. 'Ye lives like royalty,' he'd say.

Dad's friend Harry would arrive at the back door with his customary 'Whoa up!' Harry had hair like wire wool and a voice to match. Mum was never keen on Harry who didn't help his case much by always turning up before Dad's breakfast was finished. Mum saw even less of Dad at the weekends, and as Harry was his mate, it wasn't surprising that she felt the need to sweep the floor when he arrived, taking the broom right up to his feet.

'I'll wait in the lorry,' Harry would say, sloping off with a hurt expression on his face.

Harry had gone with Dad to Ireland once to see our 'Nanny Sullivan' and the family in Cork. They were late coming back and his wife had rolled up the street to complain to Mum. The strain of several days without so much as a postcard from Harry showed on her face which was flat and brown like the surface of our kitchen table. Her straight hair was prematurely streaked with grey and she wore a couple of grips to keep it back. She had yellowy brown eyes that stared at you with distrust from beneath heavy lids. Kenny, her youngest, had been in tow that day; his face was all snotty and his nappy had slipped down inside his rubber pants. It was on his bottom that his mother vented her frustration when he wouldn't let go of our swing. They were both upset without Harry, of course, and it touched something inside me. What would happen if my Dad never came home? It was a relief when he'd eventually blown in with his huge suitcase a few hours later. This same suitcase had accompanied him from Cork when he'd left to join the Air Force several years before and, although somewhat large and cumbersome, was unlikely to be traded in for a newer model. Dad's motto was 'If it ain't broke…' and even if it had been, a strap would no doubt have been applied to secure it.

Whenever he went to Ireland, Dad would bring home Killarney rock for us kids and a gift for Mum, which was once a pair of shamrock earrings. Even if he made straight for the yard on his return we were content knowing that our lynch pin was back in place.

Dad was a heavyweight boxer in his youth and was still competing when I was small. I'd never seen him in the ring, only having knockabout sessions in the backyard with local lads, but there was boxing on TV once so I knew what went on. I remember during one of Dad's absences I'd crept into the airing cupboard where some of his kit lay. Sitting amid a pile of satin shorts and head protectors, I'd slipped my hands into his gloves hoping he would win and not be hit too much. How soft those gloves were inside considering the damage they could do!

The Champeen

When Dad returned from a bout in Helsinki with an eye the colours of the lollipop he'd brought me back, I had burst into tears at the sight of him.

'Don't be making faces,' he said. 'I'm the champeen me.'

Back in those days, when he was still training, Dad would jog along the street dishing out punches to imaginary adversaries with me beside him trying to keep up.

'All right, Paddy?' people would say. 'OK, John L?'

Dad kept chickens in the back garden and often these jogs were to the seed shop on the corner of Albemarle Road. I remember the place was always warm inside with wooden bays full of different seed. The door's little flat handle was thin from years of use and at the clang of its bell the proprietor would appear. The shop was dusty from the seed and showers of coloured specks would be caught in the rays of the sun through the window. I used to think these were fairies or bits of rainbow. Once back at home, Dad would mix the seed with bread, kneading the mixture in his great fists before throwing it to the squawking chickens.

Sometimes we'd take a walk up to Willesborough mill. I remember its huge white bulk looking enormous against the sky as we approached along the overgrown path. Will was only a scrap at the time and Dad would carry him in his arms or up on his shoulders. 'Bumper boots' were all the rage then and Dad was delighted at being able to fit his awkward feet into a pair. He teamed them up with jeans that he boasted only cost half a crown in Lewis and Hylands. These were as stiff as boards until Mum softened them up in her much prized single-tub washing machine.

Later on, when he got a car, Dad would take us for the occasional 'spin' to 'Wye Crown'. The series of pathways on the Downs chiselled out into the shape of a crown had been made by students of Wye College in 1902 for the coronation of King Edward VII. We kids didn't know about all that of course; we were just fascinated to walk on the crown that you could see from miles away. There were huge, primeval-looking stones lying about in the long grass, their flinty purple surfaces catching the sun like mirrors. While we ran about, Dad would sit gazing out across Kent as though working things out in his mind. He was always trying to see how our situation could be improved upon.

**The Mill at Willesborough painted by the author
from an original photograph**

Sometimes Mum would pack a picnic and on a summer's afternoon there might only be the drone of a glider plane or the cry of a distant sheep to be heard, accompanied perhaps by Dad's own 'baaaa' after a ham sandwich.

The place had a different charm in winter for Will and myself; then the wind would steal our breath and whip our hair as we skidded along the slippery wet grass in our wellies. The descent was rather precarious and if you broke into a run there was only a flimsy wire fence to prevent you from flying onto the road beneath, but that made it all the more exciting.

Gradually the yard took precedence over everything and required Harry to pitch up quite a bit on Sunday mornings. Dad would do his best to smooth things over with Mum but he never had to try very hard.

'Whassup, Lizzie Wallace?' he'd say patting her like an affectionate grizzly bear.

Mum's name wasn't Elizabeth or even Wallace for that matter. Wallace had been Nana Spice's maiden name. She had been Joan Spice before her marriage but an Iraqi houseboy had called her Lizzie by mistake at her WAAF station and it had somehow stuck. Dad had his own nicknames for all of us - 'Lindy Lou', 'Mosie Top', 'Willie James' and 'Anno'. He also had one or two others for when we were naughty.

'Go on with you, Sullivan,' Mum would answer with a laugh. She was usually elbow deep in dishes or struggling with sheets in the single tub when Dad went to hug her. As the yard was Dad's domain, so the house was hers. They were a good team, he and she.

Mum and Dad in
London, 1952

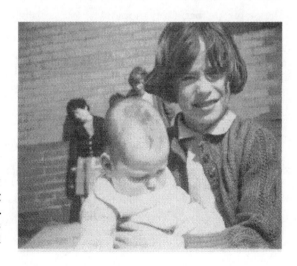

With Anne, my
Sunday morning
charge, in 1962.
Mo and playmates
in the background

Once Around the Cemetery

The square at the front of our house was always quiet on a Sunday morning as though the houses themselves were in no hurry to wake. I usually got the job of taking Anne out in the pram while Mum 'got on'.

The occasional blast of music from my friend Patty's shed would mean that her dad was at his favourite pastime, tinkering about with radios. Apart from this there was only the squeaking of the pram to be heard as I walked along, or the occasional hiss from a string of plastic teddies as Anne batted them with her fist.

If I knocked for Patty I would invariably be told that she was going out for the day to her auntie's, but it was always worth a try. More often than not though, Patty would be seen a little while later, heading off to the bus stop in Church Road with her parents; her mum in a straw hat and her dad in his grey cap and waistcoat. Patty, forced to wear a dress, would be hopping about in front like a poodle anxious to be off the lead.

I'd usually head for the cemetery and dawdle around the pathways for an hour or so until Anne dozed off. I knew that if I went back too soon I'd get involved with the Sunday chores. Pushing Anne around was preferable to that, even though she was a stubborn little madam and would fight sleep as long as she could.

A communial alleyway led from our street up into the one beyond. Here, kids biked, skated and played marbles and hopscotch until they were tall enough to see over the wall. Lovers met here at night when it was a dark and sinister. In the early morning, it was always chilly around your legs until the sun had warmed the place.

On one of my Sunday morning walks with Anne, I encountered Valerie Patterson coming towards me in the alley. We children disliked the Pattersons; there were loads of them and they always wanted to fight.

Valerie's hands were shoved down into the pockets of her school mac despite the warm weather. Like her sisters, Valerie was never seen in a pretty dresss. One side of her pink rimmed glasses was usually covered by a filthy plaster and her mouth was set in a thin line. With her good eye she gave me a hateful stare and thumped my arm for no good reason other than perhaps to lash out at life in general. I fended off another blow without letting go of the pram and moved away quickly with Valerie's dislike boring into my back as hot as the morning sun. As I got older I pitied Valerie whose mother's voice was often heard screaming 'Valerie! Mary! Kieran! Get over here now!' The kids were never in a great hurry to obey, knowing they were probably in for a smack around the head or a grasping by the hair and a marching indoors for further punishment.

If they spotted their grandmother coming along the street, the Pattersons would surround her yelping like a pack of hyenas so that she was obliged to put down her shopping bag and spread out her shaky hands out to calm them. Although we didn't like them, we always considered ourselves very lucky compared to the Pattersons.

The Church Road entrance to the cemetery was always dark, even on the brightest day. Trees met overhead and the sharp, dank smell of rotting foliage permeated the air. Near the gate was an ancient tank full of murky water for the topping up of flower pots. Watering cans were stacked here and always returned to their place beside the tank after use. People were quite obedient about this. No-one ever left them where they shouldn't be or stole them; it just didn't seem to happen.

I remember sunlight streaming through the branches and moving like a lacy blanket over the pram. Anne was forever tugging at her bonnet so that it would slip over one side of her face. I would pick at the wet, woolly knot beneath her chin in an effort to get the thing off and once had to pull it over her head from the back so that she gasped in terror thinking I was trying to suffocate her.

Anne had got off lightly in the bonnet department compared to us three elder children, who'd had to contend with Mum's knitted, all-covering helmets. The nearest thing to compare these with would be the headgear worn by Archbishop Cranmer in Elizabethan times. The helmets had been square in shape and the top corners poked up like cat ears. The hole at the front fitted snugly around our faces so that when its woollen ties were drawn, our cheeks were squashed and our foreheads pushed in to a frown. Two large pom-poms were added to the ties so we had to contend with these hanging down onto our chests into the bargain. We probably got a reputation for the unhappiest looking babies in Willesborough.

Dad wasn't wrong in declaring Anne as strong as a bullock. In her fight against sleep she would cling onto the pram sides and arch her back so that I couldn't settle her down. If I tried to dislodge her fists she would break into a yell fit to wake those beneath the grass. Mum said Anne was her biggest baby, weighing in at over nine pounds and she'd never forget her arrival on that October night in 1961 – neither would I. Mum was making so much noise that our Nana Spice came into the front room and turned the volume up on the TV. Will and I were watching '77 Sunset Strip' with Dad at the time, although it was probably only Will who was watching it as in his mind Dad would have been upstairs with Mum. That wasn't the way then though and Nana Spice was very much in charge.

I remember feeling all screwed up knowing that Mum was suffering upstairs in a way as yet unknown to me. I hadn't any idea about birth and assumed babies came out of a hole near ladies' belly buttons which was left gaping afterwards, pending stitches. In the days leading up to Anne's arrival I had come across Mum and Nan talking in furtive whispers about 'a hard time' and 'starting' and 'waters breaking.' All this left me baffled. Once, when a snippet was shown on TV of woman about to give birth, Mum had screamed and hurled herself in front of the screen, so I was still none the wiser.

I myself had been born during the early hours of the morning while an August thunderstorm raged. Mum had gone into labour after polishing off a plate of sprats at Sunday tea so that Nan was obliged to hurry across Newtown Green to phone for the ambulance. I was brought home to number 235 during an angst-ridden time, with Grandfather Spice very ill and Nan beside herself with worry. Anne, however, had come along when my parents were in their prime and life, though not without its problems, was a little more relaxed.

A small pot near the end of the path to the right of the cemetery's main route commemorated the resting place of my great-grandparents. I knew very little about them except that they had been Frank and Louisa Wallace, parents to our Nana Spice.

In later life I would discover that my great-grandfather Frank had been born in New York City and served in the Kings Royal Rifles in various campaigns in the Boar War. Somehow he had pitched up in

Frank and Louisa Wallace beside the rhubarb

Ashford married to Louisa Wood who'd been born in Aldershot and was brought up in Hothfield. While 'earwigging' conversations between Mum and Nana Spice, I would learn about Frank's quiet demeanour and Louisa's unquiet one, and how my great-grannie ran their house opposite the Broomfields like a battleship. Frank's allotment became his refuge apparently when Louisa launched campaigns of her own. A photograph on the wall in Nan's kitchen showed the two of them exchanging a smile over the rhubarb – Frank with a moustache and flat cap, Louisa in a flowered overall with her hair bound up in two rams horns either side of her head. They had five children, Nana Spice or 'Ellen', being the second eldest.

Another frequently visited memorial was that of David Evans, whose motor bike went into a wall up at the by-pass. David had sometimes served in his parents' shop at the end of our street. I remembered him being quite tall, and that his hair was dark brown with other shades through it like the colour of chestnuts and conkers when you dig them out of their spiky cases. It flopped forward like a curtain once as he leant across the counter to work out our bill. He used a red pen on a white paper bag and spoke very nicely to me saying 'Please' and 'Thank you, love.'

It was strange to think of David under that white stone on which the word 'Cariad' was etched and where fresh flowers were often placed. Once these were big tulips as red as the ink on that paper bag.

A grave under a tree near the far entrance was that of Philip who had been our playmate until he had died of cystic fibrosis. Our games would often be halted while poor Philip gave way to horrendous coughing fits. His mother, Alison, would rub his back and we would all stand about awkwardly until the bout had passed. Sometimes it didn't and we were all sent home. Alison did ladies' hair in her kitchen and made beautiful angel cakes; birthday parties for Philip and his sister were always wonderful, involving indoor games and take away lucky bags.

When Philip died, our Mum said her heart went out to Alison. During the years when he'd been in reasonable health we'd had fun with Philip and his sister who would dress their cat up and push it around in her doll's pram. It was as daft as anything, that cat, lying there in a pink romper suit. Of course, things were never the same after Philip died and the family moved away.

I nearly died once myself but I never told Mum for fear of getting Rose Drake who lived nearby into trouble. I was about four years old and we had just moved to our three-bedroomed house in Twelve Acres from a two-bedroomed one further up the estate in Breadlands Road. Rose had offered to take me on a walk with a few other bigger kids. We went to Crow Bridge where you could get down near the line before the days of electrification. Rose and the other girls in the party were on the hunt for primroses. I was learning how to distinguish these from dandelions or buttercups and spotted some growing right beside the track. Off up the grassy bank I went. After a few minutes, everyone started shouting and when I turned round I saw a train heading towards me, getting bigger by the second. I jumped and rolled down the bank, legs and flowers flying through the air. Ever since then, whenever I smell primroses, that memory is still there beyond their delicate perfume.

The cemetery was the favourite stopping off point for my sister Mo and I on the way back from our trips to the Post Office. We would sit by our great-grandparents or Philip or 'Cariad' with our Penny Arrows and Sherbert Fountains. Death didn't mean much to us then. We were sad about Philip, of course, but we'd had little to do with David aside from those odd times in the shop. Both deaths had happened when we were a couple of years younger and, because of her own circumstances, Mo hardly remembered those involved at all.

I often wondered what it might be like to have no brothers and sisters like Patty. When playing in her house I couldn't get over the fact that her toys were always in exactly the same place as she had left them the previous day. However, she had far less freedom than I due to her watchful parents. Once released from childminding, I could go wherever I wanted as long as I returned at mealtimes. It was safe to wander off as far as you liked in those days.

The ideal family set up it seemed to me back then was that of Simone at school. Her Dad came from Cork like ours and also worked in the factory. There was a big glass case in her front room containing dolls from all over the world and her bedroom was full of beautiful things. However, Simone was far more interested in doing her hair and putting on make-up than playing with dolls. She was allowed out till late and could even go up the town if she wanted. Her wardrobe was full of lovely clothes and I reckoned her dressing table set was pure magic.

'Well,' said my mum when I raved over Simone's possessions and Patty's undisturbed toys. 'They're the only ones, what do you expect?'

I had most in common with Patty so I called her my 'best friend.' Rose's sister Yvonne was OK, but she didn't like climbing trees or doing acrobatics or putting on shows for people at the drop of a hat like Patty was prepared to. All she seemed to enjoy doing was playing records on her front step and, in general, copying Rose, who was then about to be married. Being the eldest, I had no big sister to copy so instead would use TV characters for my role models like Cathy Gale on 'The Avengers.' Patty and I often played 'The Avengers' as she was very easy to throw over my hip in a judo move I had learned from watching Mrs Gale. Patty was also brilliant at climbing and we often sat on the top of my swing like a couple of chimps deciding which game to play next. We both wore those stretchy trousers with the elastic underneath the foot. Our legs were bony so it didn't take long before the knee area had its own little extension at the front and we'd be walking around like a couple of emus. Fashion wasn't on our minds then though. We were too busy having fun.

Mrs Cherry, Snails and Popcorn

One Sunday, after the usual turn around the cemetery with the pram, I decided to give a couple of dead snails a proper burial. Mo had found them on the path when she'd taken her daily few yards' walk to the square. There was a large one and a smaller one beside it, so I made a cross out of two lolly sticks tied together and chalked on it 'Susie Snail and Baby.'

Mo sat watching from the wall as I began digging the 'grave' in the front garden. This wall ran in front of the houses on two sides of the square and was a couple of feet wide. A game of 'Jump the Gap' meant clearing the space where the wall ended either side of the alley. I once slightly underestimated the gap's width and went home yelling with two grazed shins.

We were half way through the burial when Mrs Cherry from the corner house decided to come along the wall, as she often did, barefoot. Her tread was a heavy thud like Dad's on the landing in the morning and she was wearing one of her flowery summer dresses, its skirt billowing out like a mainsail. Sometimes, if it was hot, she would arrive in a halter-necked swimsuit with a frilly skirt around it. Mo and I were always interested in Mrs Cherry's clothes because she resembled a big girl dressed up.

Back then I would have described Mrs Cherry as having a wide mouth with lots of teeth in it and a hairy face like that of 'Alwyn,' her Airedale who Mo disliked due to her scratchy paws. Alwyn's predecessor, 'Buller,' had been a slow old boy much like Mr Carling, Mrs Cherry's father. A cross between an Irish Wolfhound and something very calm and curly, he had remained as steady as a rock when Dad placed Will on his back once for a ride along the path.

Mrs Cherry was always interested in our games, being, as I say, very child-like herself. She had a haircut similar to my own except that her fringe was shorter. Mrs Cherry was probably middle aged at that time, certainly older than our mother but younger than our Nana Spice. Mrs

Cherry used words like 'perfectly' and 'sickening' when she spoke to Mum sometimes by the wall about the Pattersons or the way the Council men had left the grass to blow all over the paths.

Mrs Cherry's son John had been killed while serving in Cyprus. His body was not brought home so no grave existed for us kids to sit by with our chews. I knew about this but didn't really grasp the full extent of the tragedy at that time or why Mrs Cherry studied the writing on the lolly stick for so long. I was hoping she would continue her walk to wherever she was heading. Alwyn was getting restless and heading for Mo's legs as usual. But Mrs Cherry had lain down on the wall by then with her eyes closed. I sometimes did this on tombstones up the churchyard myself and it was strange to see a grown up acting in the same way.

'Muriel!' called Mr Carling, who was making his way along the path with Mrs Carling on his arm. Mrs Carling was stiff as the stick she clutched for support and, in her bell-shaped hat, looked a bit like the standard lamp in Nana Spice's dining room. On her hands she wore fine lace gloves like the old-fashioned lady that she was.

When Mr Carling called out to Mrs Cherry, his voice sounded like Will's teddy when tipped upside down. This was appropriate really as he resembled a white old bear himself with his huge hairy ears and mouth set in a straight line. Mrs Cherry didn't deign to move from the wall until her parents were almost upon her. Then she whistled to Alwyn and off up the alley went the party; Mrs Cherry marching rebelliously in front, the two elderly folk bringing up the rear and Alwyn running back and forth between them all.

I'd been into Mrs Cherry's house once for popcorn when Mr and Mrs Carling weren't there and told Mo afterwards how different it had appeared to our own. For a start, it was very quiet apart from the loud ticking of the clock in the hall. Afterwards I'd lain on the wall out front to see if I could hear it ticking and had been quite surprised that I couldn't.

The window in the Carlings' kitchen had been open and bright nasturtiums were pushing in from the trelliswork outside. I'd stood on the mat like Mrs Cherry instructed while she went upstairs. I was to wait for her to call out 'Cooeee,' and then repeat it back to her. I imagined this was to make sure I did not move from the designated spot.

While Mrs Cherry was gone I'd had a look around as far as it was possible to do so with one foot remaining on the mat. On the dresser was a photo of John in his soldier's uniform. A flower had been placed beside it, not a nasturtium in yellow or orange, but a single white rose. There was no washing up by the sink and the wall mirror was a pretty affair with a cut glass edge, not spotted brown with the corner missing like the one Dad shaved in with his braces hanging down.

Mrs Cherry's 'Cooeee!' followed the sound of the toilet flushing so I did my best to answer, but 'Cooeee' was not a word I'd ever yelled and it came out like a parrot's caw. Mrs Cherry produced a bowl of toffee popcorn from the fridge for me to try. I told Mo that the fridge was like ours inside with the ice tray in a little slot on the right. These details from other people's homes were very important to me at that age.

'What did the popcorn taste like?' asked Mo impatiently, Mrs Cherry's fridge did not hold much interest for her.

When I said it was like toffee and paper mixed together, Mo's mouth went the way it did when Mum gave her syrup of figs and she decided she hadn't missed out on much at all.

I remember gazing over to Mrs Cherry's from our swing, wondering which bedroom window was hers and what it was like inside. I'd wanted to have a look upstairs during my brief visit, but didn't dare ask. I was often out on the swing, imagining myself as 'Katy' who hurt her back in the story. There was no chance of breaking though with our swing. Dad had welded the chains on at the top, as well as burying its four supports in concrete. No-one would be able to get it out of the ground without great difficulty. It would be there forever I decided, long after we had all grown up and gone.

To put a different perspective on the world I would lean backwards while swinging and view the garden upside down. Once I caught Mo gazing out of the front room window at me. I smiled and waved, but she didn't smile back. Of course, Mo couldn't know how it felt to be upside down on the swing and saw the world from a different perspective all the time.

Love and Marriage

Rose and Nick had been 'courting', as Mum put it, for a couple of years. Rose used to wait on the wall out the front every evening, often with me sitting beside her, until Nick rounded the corner and cut across the square. Then, the two of them would go off down the path together with their little fingers joined and Rose's slingbacks going clackity-clack. After they were married, I wondered whether they would be less approachable in their house down near the Co-op.

'Don't go round there making a nuisance of yourself,' Mum had warned. 'They're married now.'

I wondered what happened behind closed doors when people got married. Did they grow another head? And what about the mystery of Bognor Regis?

While I'd been round Drake's the night before the wedding trying on my bridesmaid's dress, one of Rose's workmates had asked if she was nervous and Rose said yes, she was.

'You will be tomorrow night, eh?' chipped in another and everyone had laughed.

'Why will she be nervous at Butlins?' I asked. 'On the advert people look like they're having fun there.'

Then everyone started screaming with laughter over their Babychams and Cherry B's, even Yvonne who was supposed to be my friend. I'd felt quite betrayed and still didn't see why Rose would have been nervous the night after the wedding was all over. What a silly thing to say, I thought to myself. Some people!

When Rose had knelt down at the altar next to Nick, the price label had been visible on one of her shoes. Someone had giggled and Mrs Drake was furious. 'I knew we'd forget something!' she'd hissed.

Rose's hand was shaking when she held it out for Nick to put the ring on. I had a wart on my own wedding finger and decided this must be the reason that Rupert, who lived next door to us and with whom I had fallen in love, did not seem to reciprocate my feelings.

'Out the way, beanpole!' he would yell if I encountered him on his bike in the alley. Communication between us got even worse after the 'letter' business. Mo said I'd cooked my own goose there but what was I supposed to do? How else would I ever have known what he thought of me? I had found out and no mistake, but still I didn't want to believe it.

I'd got the idea of writing to Rupert from one of the magazines that Mrs Drake had passed on to Mum. It was on the 'Mary Advises' page. A woman had written in about her son's shyness holding him back in life.

Could Rupert's lack of attention to me have been blamed on shyness? I'd convinced myself that it was the only possible explanation and had devised the 'letter' plan to make it easier for him to express his feelings.

'Dear Rupert,' I'd written on a piece of paper from Mum's writing pad. 'Do you love me?'

I had drawn two boxes underneath marked 'yes' and 'no' respectively with the instruction to tick the relevant one. Mo had to be taken into my confidence for the plan to be put into action as she was to be the bearer of the missive. One afternoon when Rupert was in his back garden pumping up his bike tyres, Mo had headed off down the garden path clutching the note and trying not to laugh while I'd stood trembling in the shed.

Eventually, after a few agonising minutes, I heard the familiar scrape of Mo's calliper on the path.

'What did he say?' I asked, wanting and yet not wanting to know. Mo had made no attempt to staunch her laughter.

'Where's the letter?' I screamed. 'Didn't you give it to him?'

'He threw it in the stingers,' said Mo, her face wide with mirth.

'What for?'

'He didn't want to do the boxes. He said he liked me best anyway.'

'Why?' I asked, eyes brimming.

'He said my hair's like a Greek goddess's and yours is like rats' tails.'

I never wanted to leave the shed or see Rupert again as long as I lived, which might have proved a little difficult with his house being attached to my own. How could I face him after that? I really don't know what I was expecting but I hadn't bargained for such brutality.

My humiliation wasn't to end there either. Word got back to Mum that I was 'sweet on' Rupert.

'There goes the heart throb,' she said to Mrs Barr the next morning as Rupert peddled away up the alley with a gang of school mates.

'Eh?' said Mrs Barr gathering in her milk delivery.

I ran crimson-faced across the square. I'd barely ever exchanged two words with Mrs Barr and had only ever gone round to her house once before when on being home alone, I'd almost choked on a large boiled sweet. I'd rattled the letterbox desperately and was almost blue by the time she'd finally opened the door. Without removing her cigarette, she gave me a hard thump between the shoulder blades and had gone back inside once the sweet had flown out onto the step. Her smoky laugh followed me as Mum enlightened her about my feelings for her son.

Rose and Nick's reception was held down at the Army hut where a Union Jack billowed over the door in the breeze. Mr Drake had sat smoking his roll-ups and blinking his birdy eyes at his eldest daughter in her finery. With a cigarette constantly stuck between his lips and being almost all skin and bone you wouldn't have thought he'd last the year out, but he proceeded to survive well into his eighties. Mr Drake's neck was so thin that there was quite a lot of room between it and the collar of his new white shirt. I said as much to Mum at the table but she told me not to be rude and remember the scooter he'd made me and Will's go-kart.

When Rose cried at the reception, I was quite taken aback. To me, Rose was always completely in control. I'd watched through 'Carola's' window as she had deftly covered old ladies' heads with rollers and bossed the other girls about.

Earlier on her wedding day, she had sat passing pins and instructions to the girls for the hairstyle that she'd gone for – a French roll topped off with curls. It had been funny to see Rose having her own hair tinkered with for a change while I underwent my first shampoo and set. The headdress, a white circular band which was to encompass the whole creation, had been on and off a dozen times before Rose was content for it to be pinned at last and lacquered. I'd seen the girls exchanging conspiratorial glances over her head throughout the operation, but who could blame her wanting perfection on her wedding day?

At the reception, after several drinks, the Carola girls had become loud and started banging the table and tapping glasses until Rose had been forced to make some kind of speech. She began by thanking her mum for all she'd done; and promptly burst into tears. Our mum said she wasn't surprised. She might have had to wash up at her own wedding but at least she'd never had to speak, apart from during the service and that was bad enough. She said that lot from Carola should have known better and she doubted the same would have happened with the girls at 'La Parisienne,' her own hairdressers up town which was different place altogether.

'You mustn't cry on your wedding day, duck,' soothed our mum as Mrs Drake produced a handkerchief from her handbag and passed it to Rose.

'No, there'll be plenty of time for that afterwards,' yelled some wag from further down the table, earning him a mouthful from Mrs Drake. It then went a bit quiet until Nick's friend, the 'Best Man', stood up and talked about Nick at school and Nick at his work and people clapped and laughed out loud. Mr Drake stood up after that with his tie undone and his collar loosened even further and said something we couldn't make out due to the roll-up which he did not remove even for this. Rose and Nick posed for photographs as they cut the cake. Nick put his hand over Rose's pointed sleeve and Rose gave a 'Tangerine Ice' smile. That was her lipstick colour – 'Tangerine Ice.' I'd seen it in its gold case on the kitchen table at Mrs Drake's on the Friday night. Mrs Drake chose this moment to dive forward and adjust Rose's veil thereby blocking the couple with her ample turquoise duster coat and spoiling the first photo entirely.

'Never mind,' said the photographer with a frozen smile.

On the walk back after the reception we stopped off at Rose's new home, carrying the wedding gifts from the hut. I had care of the Pyrex measuring jug. The men stood chatting in the hall while the ladies had a good look round courtesy of Mrs Drake.

'Rose won't mind,' she said proudly opening doors and cupboards for examination. There were murmurs of 'Nice and clean' and 'Handy for the shops.' There was some 'ah-ing' at a picture of Nick and Rose on the mantel. The two of them had gone off in a taxi by then up to the station and whatever it was that lie in wait for them at Bognor Regis.

'Remember how we started off, Sull?' I overheard Mum say as we all filed back down the path.

'My Jaysis,' said Dad, as though he remembered only too well.

From earwigging I had learned of Mum and Dad's difficulties when they were first married. Fresh out of the forces, they had encountered some opposition on both sides, Dad because his chosen mate wasn't

Irish or Catholic at least, and Mum for returning from the WAAF, not with Bob Smurthwaite, who had been on his way to becoming 'something in the City' prior to joining up, but our dad.

Mum had enlisted at nineteen in order to 'see a bit of the world.' After a reluctant posting away from her mates in Kasfareet, Egypt to Habbaniya, near Baghdad, she'd gone to see a boxing match one evening. Having watched a handsome Irish heavyweight knock his opponents to the canvas she had been floored herself when he'd approached afterwards with a pie and asked if she 'wanted a bite.'

The two were forced to spend some time apart after their wedding before they found a house of their own. Mum continued to live at home as Granddad Spice had been diagnosed with cancer. Prior to joining the railway, Dad lived in at his hotel job in London.

'Your Dad and I weren't even together there,' said Mum once when we were looking at the few snaps she had of her own special day. 'Look at that.'

Sure enough, the rather bewildered looking Parish priest of the time had somehow managed to insinuate himself between the newly-weds.

'He was all over the place,' said Mum. 'For all I know, we might not be properly married at all. Still...bit late now.'

Mum and Dad's wedding, November 1952

Pin-ups

Our house would smell of cabbage long after the Sunday lunch plates were back on the shelf and Dad had returned to the yard.

'Cabbage is good for you,' Mum would say as we turned up our noses at the table. 'No cabbage, no pudding.'

Sunday tea time was much more relaxed because you didn't have to eat everything that was put out like spring onions if you hated them or mustard pickle. As long as you had a couple of paste sandwiches, you were entitled to a slice of the apple pie that had been baking like a poultice all afternoon. There was custard or 'Carnation' when milk supplies were running low. The standing joke was that by the time the pan got round to me, last to be served, there'd be very little left. Mum would scrape the saucepan or shake the dregs from the tin while I sat there unimpressed.

'Sorry, love,' she'd say stifling a laugh while no-one else bothered to. 'You can have most next time.'

Sunday lunch was prepared as 'Two-Way Family Favourites' played in the background. There was 'Jean in London,' 'Bill in Cologne,' and Mum in the kitchen.

'That's really square,' said Yvonne from her front step once as strains of Matt Monroe's 'Softly' emanated from our house. She would play her records on a Dansette plugged in to the hall light socket. Everything was 'square' to Yvonne apart from the likes of the Everley Brothers and Adam Faith, who she referred to as 'dreamy.'

One day, not long after Rose's wedding, Mrs Drake appeared at the front door with a paper bag full of pin-ups removed from Rose's bedroom wall.

'You can have these if you want, duck,' she said. 'Otherwise, they're going in the dustbin.'

I didn't know who the bequiffed idols were apart from Cliff and Elvis, who were always on the radio and whose songs were played down the club or by Yvonne. We had a record player in our house, not a

Dansette, but a great clumsy thing in the corner of the front room. However, it was still an improvement on the squeaky old gramophone we'd had in Breadlands Road. Singers like Elvis weren't played on it until a few years later when 'In The Ghetto' somehow managed to slip through Dad's net of Irish ballads and Jim Reeves. Dad made up his own lyrics to the song:

And a hungry little boy with a snotty snout,
Plays in the street with his arsehole hanging out
In the ghettooooooo

Dad liked Scottish music too and would sing along with Andy Stewart and Kenneth McKellar on the White Heather Club when he was getting ready to go out. He was fond of 'My Love is Like a Red, Red Rose' and would bounce on the balls of his curly feet to 'Donald Where's Yer Troosers,' a bath towel wrapped around his middle.

When I spread the collection of pin-ups across table for Mum to see, she pointed out Billy Fury, Jess Conrad, Buddy Holly, Bobby Vee, Rock Hudson and a terrifyingly ugly man called Oliver Reed that I put straight in the dustbin.

Mum said that none of these could compare with Dad who was a very handsome man and her own favourite pin-up, although Elvis wasn't bad she had to admit. Dad was combing his hair in the kitchen mirror at the time. He tried to make it into a quiff using extra Brylcreem but it didn't quite work, so he smoothed it back down again. When Mum took a shine to Tom Jones a few years later, Dad coincidentally grew his sideburns down and when she began avidly watching 'Kojak', he was often seen driving his lorry with a lollipop at the corner of his mouth.

Before

Our move to the house in Twelve Acres from the smaller one in Breadlands Road had been pretty basic operation. I know that a cart had been involved somewhere because I remember following along behind it.

Dad soon busied himself with his dubious DIY skills and I was absolutely terrified when I found him painting the landing walls while balancing on a railway sleeper slung across the top of the stairs. This was in the days before non-drip paint and it seemed to be everywhere. It ran from the wall onto the skirting and down Dad's arm each time he raised it to slap on another brushful. By the time he'd finished, Dad looked like something off a Christmas cake. Bless.

Many of the houses on the estate had been built by German prisoners of war and all had the same substantial brick sheds. My memories of our first house in Breadlands Road were of green doors and lino on the floor where Mo and I played most of the time. I would ride my three-wheeler bike out in the garden and chase a white hen called Sheila.

Back in those early days, I was quite sure that everything in the world was geared around myself and my family and that all the songs on the radio were for us alone. 'Behind the Green Door' must surely have meant those in our kitchen and Ella Fitzgerald's 'Summertime' was all about our walks across the fields in the evenings. There was even a song about me, I decided; Paul Robeson's 'Mah Lindy Lou.'

Dad's voice would carry through the house when he sang along to Harry Belafonte's 'Island in the Sun' or 'Stand Up and Fight' to the music from 'Carmen.' Mo and I played happily together; our toys were a spinning top, some clothes pegs, a large flour sifter and my treasured black doll Susie, who had appeared one Christmas complete with earrings. Will's high chair folded down into something resembling a train and although she couldn't climb on as a fellow passenger, Mo would latch on with a finger and off we'd go, flying up to London like the 'Golden Arrow.' Outside, our chickens pecked and flapped, the living was easy like the words of 'Summertime,' or so it seemed to me back then. Of course I had no idea of the suffering that was going on above my head.

Mo had fallen victim to polio when she was only three months old. How she had caught it no-one really knew but there had been an epidemic at the time. The doctor was called and dismissed her illness as a severe cold. Unfortunately, this developed into pneumonia; Mo was taken into hospital and put in an iron lung. She woke paralysed and was diagnosed with the terrible, muscle-wasting disease. However, I saw nothing strange in the fact she was still shuffling around the floor on her bottom in her little zip-up boots long after she ought to have been walking, nor did it strike me as unusual that she rolled toys about with her chin or picked them up in her teeth instead of her hands. It was shortly after our move to the house in the square that life began to change quite drastically for all of us.

In the shed where I had stood waiting on the day of my letter to Rupert were several old forgotten things. Dad's boxing ball had peeped out from behind a pile of lumber ever since the days when he had given lessons to local lads in the back yard. There had been 'right hooks' and 'left hooks' and talk of 'John L' and 'Sugar Ray' as the ball had swung to and fro.

There were items on the shed's dusty shelf that had probably been there long before we had moved in. Rusting saws, grimy old bottles and several puncture repair kits made up the display beneath the cobwebs. Dad seldom threw anything away and neither did Mum for that matter. A puncture-ridden inner tube, coiled like a snake, had lived there for years, long after the bike it was intended for had been dumped. It couldn't be thrown out though or cut and used as a snake in a game of 'Jungle' because Dad knew it was there and would be asking for it when you were least expecting to be grilled over its whereabouts.

An old tin further along the shelf had played its part in bringing about the change to our lives. As its faded brown pattern had once been bright flowers, Mo's body had once been that of a normal child. One afternoon in 1958, powerless to stop herself, she had fallen head first from a chair right onto this tin cutting her mouth so that it poured with blood and set us all screaming.

Mum knew this was the painful answer to months of indecision. The authorities had assured her and Dad that sending Mo to Chailey Heritage, a hospital school for handicapped children would be for the best. At Chailey, Mo would learn how to walk and take care of herself, thereby gaining a degree of independence. However, the prospect of parting with three year old Mo had been too much for my parents, then only in their early twenties, to contemplate.

In the midst of all the chaos, I ran to find my father thinking he would know what to do. After all, he could mend my doll's arms when they fell out, he could stop tears and make things better like the time I fell off my bike and had blood all down my leg. Hadn't I forgotten the pain of sliding along the path on my knee when he'd jogged home with me on his back?

I stopped short at the front room door feeling like I'd been hit in the chest by the boxing ball. My brave, wonderful father was doubled up in the armchair crying his eyes out.

Mo at Chailey in 1958

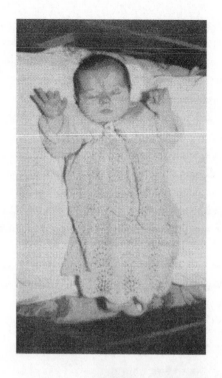

Mo at two weeks old in
1955 before tragedy
struck

Myself with Dad and Mo
in Breadlands Road

After

Although I always loved to see Mo, I never enjoyed the trip to Chailey Heritage as the duration of the visit was always overshadowed by the inevitable 'goodbyes.' In spite of the marvellous work done at the hospital school where handicapped children were taught to overcome their disabilities, it was an austere place with a tough regime. A few years later, some of the Thalidomide victims would join Mo there. It was sad to see them on visiting day with little hands flapping from their torsos like fledgling birds; Mo of course, saw them all as individuals and friends.

'This is so and so, and that one's such and such,' she would say. Most of the children seemed cheerful enough and lived up to the institution's motto, 'Laetus Sorte Mae' – 'Happy With My Lot.' Of course, at their young age they couldn't have known exactly what their 'lot' was or how it would affect the rest of their lives.

The journey to Chailey involved a train to London, the Underground to Victoria and another train from there to Haywards Heath, from where we took a bus. By the time we got to Chailey it was almost time to come back. If we went by road, the two hour trip was often dogged with misadventure due to either Will or myself being car sick or the breaking down of whichever unreliable vehicle Dad was driving at the time. Over the years these included an adapted hearse, a British Rail parcel lorry (cab and base only, which to save embarrassment had to be secreted in a wooded area with the rest of the journey completed on foot) and an old Ford complete with step boards that looked like something from an Al Capone movie. However, this would have made a poor getaway vehicle as it ground to a halt miles from anywhere.

On that particular occasion Mum, in her new white coat, had to get out and push with Dad while Will and I watched from the rear window. We screamed as the car gathered speed on a downward incline. Dad then broke into a run and leapt into the driver's seat, ripping his new waistcoat on the window handle at the same time. Much swearing and gnashing of teeth ensued when, once again, the car shuddered to a halt. Mum, who had been left behind, did not appear round the corner for some time. When she did finally arrive with her white coat only slightly stained with grease, she found us hysterical thinking we would never see her again and Dad exhausted from turning the starting handle countless times. The engine, however, had finally groaned into life.

Mum would put together a picnic for the journey. She once made jelly in flowered paper cups and placed them carefully into a little suitcase. This was in the days before the cool bag of course and that journey was particularly bumpy. When we stopped on a grass verge to eat, she was dismayed to find the case awash with raspberry and orange. Will and I scooped the jelly up laughing our heads off.

Myself and Mo at the park in 1957

The Fountain, Victoria Park painted by the author

As mentioned, leaving Mo was always traumatic no matter what brave faces we all put on. There were tears and wrenching of hearts as we departed for the bus or our vehicle while a little curly haired figure grew smaller in the distance. To us children, it seemed so unfair that Mo couldn't come home too. As we got older we understood the reasons for her being sent away and the torment involved.

During the winter months we would arrive back to find the house absolutely freezing. Dad would chop kindling wood, which was often damp and filled the place with smoke. He once threw petrol on and flames leapt up with a great roar, causing Mum to panic that the chimney would catch fire. Dad's answer was to roar too, but with laughter.

There was no hot water until the geyser had been lit. Mum would boil saucepans and give us a wash down in front of the fire. Lying on the sofa in our pyjamas watching 'Sunday Night at the London Palladium,' Will and I would talk about Mo in her bed with bars on and all the little kids at Chailey with no arms and legs and think ourselves very lucky indeed.

Mo, Park Trips and Nana Spice

When she came home for holidays, Mo would need time to become acclimatised. As Mum swapped her shoes and calliper for slippers, she would look around, remarking on any little changes like new wallpaper, a different tablecloth or a new rug. Everything underfoot had to be negotiated for her safety, but it was Mum rather than Mo who flew through the air one morning when she caught her slipper on an upturned corner of a new plastic mat!

Mo usually sat on an upright chair for back support while Mum put tea in front of her. Sometimes she cried at this point; no-one needed to ask why. The cosiness of home and the simple act of being served tea by Mum rather than a nurse or ward orderly was enough to start her off. This would be a kind of turning point, after which she would begin to settle in.

Mo was proud to be able to do many things for herself like her washing her face and brushing her teeth. She would perform a trick with her left arm which was to swing it round fast from her shoulder like a propeller.

'Do it again!' Will and I would say. Mo would be quite happy to oblige, making a joke of it which was always her way.

People were always stopping in the street to say how much Mo looked like Mum. It was true for they both had the same dark curls. However, Mo was never happy with her hair and used to get cross when Mum brushed it up. 'You look just like a little dolly,' she'd say. Scowling, Mo would lift her 'good' hand by biting on a piece of elasticated material around her wrist and proceed to push the curls as flat as she could.

'It's not modern,' she'd say. 'I hate it!'

Now and then, on a fine day, we'd make the two mile walk to Victoria Park. When Will was a baby, Mum would push the pram with Mo sitting on top in a little white seat. By the time Anne arrived, Will was big enough to walk and I'd push Mo in her chair. All would be fine on the outward journey but Will would usually have a 'paddy' on the way home, complaining that his legs were aching. He'd stomp along behind us flapping his arms. One afternoon he started kicking the cinema wall for all he was worth and, surprised at coming off worse, yelled even louder.

If we had to wait at the crossing for a train to pass, Mum would keep us amused with a tale about a lump of coal that had fallen from a steam train onto a lady's pram and how lucky it was that only the blanket was burned and not the baby. Standing on the bridge as the train flew under was exciting. The bridge itself seemed to lift a little with the force of it and the noise made you want to scream out loud.

Eventually, the crossing man would emerge from his little wooden hut to open the gates. Through the hut's open door a kettle could be seen on a low table and a pair of gingham curtains hung in the window. It was a bit like the 'club' we'd once had in Philip's shed, but this one belonged to a grown up so it was all the more intriguing to glimpse its interior.

After crossing the track with the train growing smaller in the hazy distance, we'd turn into Newtown Road. Flanked on one side by boards the route was became known as just that, 'The Boards.'

The paddling pool at Victoria Park was a concrete rectangle full of weeds and small stones, but that didn't bother the boys in their shorts or the girls like me with their dresses tucked into their knickers. All we wanted to do was pull our shoes and socks off and get in. Kids massed around the sides like starlings, while parents sat on the grass or pushed swings and held little ones onto see-saws.

Across the park stood an elaborate fountain made up of two male and two female figures holding discs above their heads. Water now tumbles down but back then it was always dry. To climb into the laps of these stone giants and gaze into their dead eyes was fascinating. Their huge limbs were beautifully crafted and at their feet were several gaping fish in the same dark stonework. Three small cherubs stood at the fountain's pinnacle as though on lookout. There had once been a bandstand and Mum told us how people would sit in deckchairs listening to the music when she was brought to the park as a child before the war.

At school someone in our class had boasted that they'd been a 'war baby.' The war having been over a good seven years before any of us in Class Two had been born, the title could only have belonged to much older brothers and sisters. However, back then it had seemed a very exciting thing to have been and surely meant wearing a tiny uniform and a little tin hat as your mother clutched you in the 'hair raid' shelter.

Mum put things into perspective when she told us of her experiences during the war and how it had changed everyday life so profoundly. Local men joined up and some were never seen again, leaving women to raise families alone. Ashford was a target due to the railway and there were casualties following the air raids. Nana Spice had lost her last child and blamed having to hide beneath the kitchen sink at the approach of a 'Doodle Bug' when she was eight months' pregnant.

Like many local children, Mum had been evacuated out of Ashford for safety. After a tearful goodbye at the station she had gone off to Manchester clutching her case and a box housing her gas mask.

**Uncle Bernard (front row, second right) with the Newtown
Spotting Team in 1944 after coming second in the
All England AC Recognition Test.**
(Photograph courtesy of the Kent Messenger)

Meanwhile at night, dog fights took place over the sleepy streets of Newtown. Like many young boys, my two uncles, Bernard and John found this quite exciting and would hunt for shrapnel in the gardens next day. When he was older, my Uncle Bernard joined the Newtown 'Spotters' team which operated from the roof of the bath house and was placed Number Two in the All England Aircraft Recognition Test.

On those sunny afternoons at the park, it was hard to imagine the night sky lit with fighter planes and terrified people running for cover like in the old blitz footage you saw on TV. It all seemed far away and long ago to me as I lay on the grass listening to Mum talk of war. The only screams to be heard then were those of children splashing each other in the paddling pool.

Mum often took photographs of us with an old box camera. These would take about two weeks to come through at the local chemist's. We would walk down the road laughing at ourselves squinting out in black and white.

At twenty past four, the railwaymen would emerge like bats out of the factory gates, some on bikes, some on foot, their boots scraping along the pavement as they filled the street with their clamour. Mum hated being caught up in all this so if it looked as though we may not get past the factory gate before the hoards spilled out, we'd make a detour to Nana Spice's for a cup of tea. The back door was usually open in fine weather, with Nan's stockings set out on a chair to dry. The kitchen, dark due to the tall fencing outside always smelled of gas and Camay soap.

'Always keep yourself clean,' was Nan's motto, or one of them anyway. Another was 'Never be a nuisance.'

Occasionally, Nan would allow us into her front room. This was only opened a few times each year and always held a sense of mystery due to access being so limited. Stories of the past were exchanged over our heads as we played on the carpet. I learned how our grandfather had spent his last few weeks in this room, how his awful 'death rattle' had come to an abrupt halt one August night in 1953 and how if he hadn't given up his job in the Kennington chalk pits 'he might still be around.' Then there was the story of his mother, Great-Grannie Spice, who after years of loneliness and despair had carried out her threat of putting her head in the gas oven a few days before Christmas in 1946 thereby 'breaking Grandfather's heart.'

Nana Spice (Ellen) with May in the pram, 1914

We'd be given books by Nan to keep us occupied along with warnings over messing about with ornaments or spilling our tea. Inattentiveness could result in your plate being grabbed out of your hand with a 'Fondant Fancy' only half eaten and deposited into the sink without further notice. Mo's tea would be served to her personally in a willow patterned saucer. Nan blowing on it first would provoke a titter from us and set Nan herself all of a dither.

Nan would sometimes talk about Mum as a child. It was interesting to imagine our mother in her young days. Bernard, her eldest brother, was indulged due to his cleverness and John because he was the baby of the family. Mum had helped around the house and run errands. At school she was shy and 'wouldn't say boo to a goose.'

Of her own schooldays, Nan said she didn't remember much except that she often had to take her baby sister May along while her mother took in people's washing. Nan would leave May's pram parked in the playground during lessons. Now and again the teacher would call 'Ellen Wallace, your baby's crying.'

'It's a wonder I learned anything at all,' Nan would say, but she must have picked up some education for she was an intelligent person. Like many women of her generation, she didn't get the opportunities in life to better herself. All she could hope for was to meet a decent man, marry and raise a family. This is more or less what happened after she got talking to Percy James Spice, a quiet fellow who would appear now and then in the bar at the George Hotel where Nan, as young Ellen Wallace, had taken a job to escape from life in service.

When quiet returned to the streets after the spill out from the factory, Nan would wave us off from the back gate. I wouldn't have realised it then of course, but looking back, I feel Nan gave me something to take with me every time I saw her, a little snippet of her life to keep forever. I'm pleased to say I have quite a few of these in my collection.

Summer Fun and Games

We never went away on holiday as such but during the 'factory fortnight' Dad would take us on a day out now and then or swimming in 'the Cut', a section of the River Stour which ran through the back of Newtown and South Willesborough. The trip got off to a bad start one afternoon when he couldn't find his sandals. Bent to the shape of his feet, they had been purchased in Baghdad during his RAF days.

'Looks like you walked home in them,' Mum had once quipped.

After a room to room search had turned up nothing, we set off down the road with Dad in his work boots. It was a blazing hot day and the tar on road looked as though it might melt and stick to our sandals. I remember the smell of coal dust from the railway was particularly strong in the heat. We crossed the tracks and pushed our way through the fields banked with musky elderflower. By the time we got to the river, we were eager to get into the water. Dad then emerged from the bushes where he'd been changing; his woolly trunks were peppered with holes.

'Oh dear,' said Mum. 'They must have got the moth.'

Dad tried to walk with nothing on his feet. Tottering and swearing with pain at the sharp stones, he was forced to put his work boots back on which made us giggle even more.

Eventually he lowered himself down to begin his own version of 'the Crawl,' which involved much splashing and gasping for breath as he passed to and fro behind the bullrushes like a Great White.

The afternoon passed peacefully enough until Dad put an old rubber life jacket on Will to get him used to the water. The plan went belly-up, literally, when Will panicked in the far too large life jacket and could not right himself. He had gone just a little beyond Dad's reach and was heading for the waterfall downstream. Dad launched himself in pursuit and there was a lot of screaming and water flying about, after which Will had to be soothed with cuddles, squash and a lemon curd sandwich. Apparently the episode didn't put him off water for life as he is now a qualified scuba diver.

On another scorching day, Dad took us off to 'Dreamland' at Margate, his sandals having been located at last in the bottom of the pyjama cupboard behind the kitchen door. Dreamland was a rare treat and we were crazy with excitement. We climbed into Dad's latest car and seated ourselves amongst petrol cans, newspapers a couple of saws, a sledgehammer and an old back axle. The dubious transport farted its way out of the square with us all chattering excitedly in the back.

'Grand day altogether,' Dad observed as we drove through the nodding hedgerows.

'You don't feel sick, do you?' Mum asked periodically. 'For goodness sake, tell me if you do.'

We tried not to give way to nausea but it was difficult, particularly on the way home with the excitement of Dreamland behind us and the sun blasting through the windows. Added to which, we were being slowly asphyxiated with fumes from the detritus on the floor

'My Jaysis! I dunno why I bothers me head wich ye at all,' grumbled Dad once, as Will hung out of the door retching into the grass. 'Ye can stop at home tomorrer, ye bastard nuisances.'

'Oh, Sull! All that old smelly old junk in the back, it's no wonder!'

Dad then put his foot down and swore quite a bit at the oncoming traffic while the guilty party sat ashen-faced in the back.

However, these visits to Dreamland were always worth the aggro. Dad would bellow with laughter as we plunged downwards after a creaky ascent on the 'Big Dipper' the way he did when 'Laurel and Hardy' were on TV. Mum said that when they went to the cinema during their courting days he would almost yank the seat in front out in hysteria when these films were on. Hopefully, its poor occupant was enjoying the show as much.

I loved gliding through dark tunnels in the Rainbow Tubs or colliding on the Bumper Cars as sparks flew overhead. We hated hearing the whiny siren which signified that a ride was over. Naturally, we wanted to do everything all over again and couldn't appreciate that Dad's pocket was not bottomless.

As children, to be taken out on any kind of treat was a luxury. The rest of the time, like most kids on our street, we were left to amuse ourselves. One of our favourite games was 'Hospitals' and I always felt that we had an insider's view with Mo around. She could bring 'Emergency Ward Ten' to life in our back yard. 'Emergency Ward Ten' was a TV favourite on Friday evenings and the sight of scissors and scalpels flashing across the screen to urgent music at the start of the programme was enough to have us all glued. Nan was a fan too and would exchange notes with Mum on her Saturday afternoon visit especially when 'Michaela' had her baby. *('Oooh, did you see it? Took me back.')*

Having cast herself as 'Matron,' Mo would always take part in operations despite her elevated status. I would be 'Nurse Carol Young' and Will, if around, was 'Les Large' or a porter along with Mick when necessary. Quite often though they would get fed up and disappear leaving the poor 'patient' abandoned on the trolley which was usually Will's go-kart.

Playing hospitals and watching it on TV was one thing, but when I'd had my tonsils out at seven years old I thought the end of the world had come. I remember Dad taking me into Willesborough hospital where a nurse shut me in a toilet and told me to 'make some water.' If she'd just said 'Have a pee' it would have been a lot simpler. As it was, I tried to turn on old tap at the end of a long, bandaged up pipe but couldn't manage it. I was very anxious that I hadn't been able to do as the nurse asked. 'Why couldn't she make her own water?' I wondered, especially when there was a large sink at the end of the ward?

The first day was horrible with kids like myself bawling through fear and homesickness. Being held captive indoors was a nightmare and having to wear pyjamas all the time rendered you even more helpless. Nurses bossed us around and ignored my constant questioning as to when I could go home. The day and night dragged on until finally the next morning, they came for me. I was given something like jam on a spoon to make me drowsy. It tasted foul. I remember being in the operating theatre and a rubber mask being placed over my face like at the dentist when I'd had a tooth out.

'They gassed you, that's all.' said Mo, authoritatively, when I related my traumatic experience. 'I've been gassed loads of times and cut open.'

This was true of course. Mo had undergone various operations in an attempt to straighten out her poor body. My hospital sojourn had been traumatic, but I knew it was small potatoes compared to what she'd had to put up with.

Bedtime Stories

At night, we would lie awake listening for the 'clip-clop' of Dad's shoes across the square. Dad would always be in good humour when he returned from the club down the road. He liked a few pints but had little regard for over-indulgence or wastefulness. His feelings of disgust for those who staggered home from the club on a Saturday night were often made clear.

'Look at that nanny goat,' he would say. 'Hasn't got the brains he was born with.'

Sometimes Dad would arrive bearing gifts and throw chocolate treats up the stairs to us. My favourite was the 'Fry's Five Centre,' Mo's was 'Aero' and Will loved 'Crunchie' which he would chomp no matter how tired he was so that Mum often had to cut honeycomb out of his hair the next morning.

This night-time munching played hell with our teeth and I remember Will having to visit the dentist quite a bit. Unusually, by today's standards, Dolly Mixtures were available to all children afterwards. However, instead of taking a few from those offered, Will decided his suffering was greater than most and proceeded to exit with the entire bowl under his arm until Mum managed to wrest it from him.

Dad would often regale us with a tale or two on his way to bed. There was usually a joke at the end of each one which would have us in stitches.

'How many sides has a cup?' he asked one night and on receiving no response answered himself, 'Two – the inside and the outside.'

Roaring at his own joke, Dad returned again a few seconds later with another gem.

'Did ye hear about the fella who went to the hospital with his hands all busted?' he once asked.

'No,' said we in anticipation.

" 'Doctor,' said the fella. 'Look at me hands all busted. I caught them in a machine.'"

'Sure, that's terrible but I'll soon have them fixed for yer,' says the doctor.

'Ah, that's great,' says the fella. 'But will I be able to play the piano after?'

'Ye will of course,' says the doctor. 'No doubt about that at all.'

'That's marvellous,' says the fella. 'I couldn't play it before!' "

His jokes were very predictable of course but somehow it didn't matter. We still laughed our heads off at Dad's enthusiasm rather than the joke itself. Off he would go to bed, chuckling his way along all the landing until Mum told him to shut up.

If Dad had no jokes to offer, he would tell us about himself as a child in Ireland where life was so hard that he had to share a bed with two of his brothers and go to school in an old pair of boots with no laces in. He told us how school was tough and people got the stick or the strap if they didn't behave, and how Jack, the family dog, once hopped on the bus and took himself off to town. Best of all, Mo liked the story of how he found her in a box in the snow. This story must have been handed down somewhere along the line as one of our little nieces once referred to Mo as having been adopted. Mo was rather affronted to say the least!

Those times with Dad were precious because, apart from the holiday trips which grew fewer as the yard grew busier, we would see little of him throughout the day. It was his way of touching base and usually occurred when Mo was home especially. The rest of the time he would be too exhausted to enter into much nocturnal banter with Will and I, who had school next day.

Dad once returned from a 'bouncing' job at a hotel with leftovers on a paper tray. The four of us, Dad, Will, Mo and myself massed around it like a flock of seagulls.

'Anyone would think we starved you!' said Mum encountering the empty tray beneath her slipper the following morning. But of course, the tasty midnight snack aside, it was the attention from Dad sitting on the landing like a big child himself that we enjoyed. I remember being very cross at having slept through a feast of fish and chips one night before Mo's imminent return to Chailey. However, I appreciated that

Mo's time with Dad was limited. It would be months before she would see him again. Although whole days might go by when I would barely set eyes on him myself, somewhere in the night I would feel reassured at hearing his voice, even if it were only in the form of a snore.

Sometimes I would wait for Dad at the little window on the stairs. One night a strange thing happened. I imagined I heard the wind whistling eerily around the street like it often did in the middle of winter, yet it was summertime and the bushes in the garden were unmoved. I forgot all about this until I heard the sound again on another summer night many years later in a place and situation too painful to write about here in these happy childhood reminiscences.

Often, I would lie awake listening to the sound of the railway trucks in the distance. They'd rattle along happily and then there'd be a commotion as though the front one had stopped suddenly and all the others had run into each other. I compared it to doing the Conga down the club when the front person crashed into a table and everyone buckled behind them. It was reassuring to know that wheels were still turning and life went on at the factory even after you'd fallen asleep.

Shopping and Fishing

Mo and I were regularly sent off down to the shops with a list in Mum's neat sloping print. The 'tater' bag would be on Mo's lap with her working arm stretched across it. We'd head off up the alley and the morning air would smell of earth and the newness of the day. If there had been rain overnight, the hedges would be hung with 'diamond necklaces' and the pavements would steam with drying puddles.

I would often give Mo a demonstration of how I could turn over on the sign at the end of 'Mill View.' She would indulge my whim and roar with laughter if I had difficulty righting myself as happened once when a puddle lay beneath.

We always stopped to see the tortoise in one of the gardens in Osborne Road. The tortoise was never immediately visible, but would eventually appear from beneath the rhubarb or a camouflage of twisted old roots if we waited long enough. Fascinated by its sheer ugliness, we decided it looked like a wizened old man moving along in a rubber ring. Mo reckoned it would take a whole year to reach the Co-op if it was set down on the path.

The butcher's shop was my least favourite port of call, with the cold dead creatures suspended on hooks in purple, blue and red. Invariably, a pig's head complete with eyelashes and a vague half-smile would be perched in the middle of the window display as if to say 'Yeah, horrible, isn't it? Enjoy.'

The floor of the butcher's shop was patterned in mosaic much like Sainsbury's up town. When serving ladies, the butcher would whistle and show off, throwing the purchases onto the scales from about two feet away.

'Just over, darlin', OK?' he once said to a woman in front of me with backcombed hair and white legs. 'Better too much than not enough, eh? We don't want that, do we?'

The woman had giggled and held out one of those plastic string bags which could slim to nothing until filled when it would take on the shape of its contents. I didn't see what was so amusing about 'just over' but then I didn't know about flirting and was still puzzling over Bognor Regis.

When it was my turn the mince was whipped from the scales and wrapped up in one deft movement. The pencil was taken from behind the butcher's ear and the total written on a bill beneath a picture of a ram's head. The bill, like the butcher's nails was stained with blood.

'Anything else, luvvy?' he asked.

I copied the woman's giggle to see what would happen.

'Off you go then, eh?' said the butcher maintaining a rather worried smile as I backed out grinning at him maniacally.

'He thinks you're mental,' said Mo who had been observing through the window.

Enid often served us in the Co-op. Enid lived across the square and owned Matey, a large, boisterous Labrador cross. She was mother to Monica who was away most of the time dancing with Bluebell Troupe and foster-mother to a girl called Hilary during the holidays. We always remembered Mum's instructions to say 'please' and 'thank you' as Enid filled our bag with spuds, cabbage, marmalade, Anchor butter, Rich Tea biscuits, cream crackers, Lifebuoy soap and Daz. But we had our own reasons for being polite; Enid would sometimes put a couple of bars of Nestles chocolate in with our order; usually when we were together. I didn't get much when I shopped alone, no matter how much I might fawn.

Groceries on 'tick' were forbidden. Dad liked everything paid for. 'If we can't afford it we go without,' was his motto. Mum once bought a much needed carpet sweeper from the Kleeneze man and hid it behind the kitchen door. I was sworn to secrecy with a miniature tin of polish and a tiny duster for my doll until Mum confessed to Dad about the 'Bex Bissell.' By this time the sweeper had fluff round its brushes from where Mum had tried it out and so could not be returned. When Dad saw how clear of fleck the carpet was he forgave Mum for splashing out on 'an unnecessary expense' when there was a perfectly good dustpan and brush in the cupboard.

We often stopped to peer through Carola's window at Rose working but she was always very busy and only had time for a brief wave. When she had first started there she would nip out and say hello.

'I expect she's come down to earth with a bump now the honeymoon's over,' said Mum. 'It's not all honey, especially when the kids start coming along. She won't have time for hairdressing then or much else come to that.'

I wondered if this marriage lark wasn't a little over-rated. It seemed you had to make the most of your wedding day as life afterwards seemed rather bleak.

The Post Office in Church Road was our favourite shop. The only drawback was that its doorway wasn't wide enough for Mo's chair so she had to be left outside with prams and tied up dogs. There were two parts to the Post Office; the first was a shop with sweets on one side and grocery on the other, the second was the Post Office itself where Mr Henry peered out from behind the grille to issue stamps and family allowance.

The counter there was packed with such items as postcards, glue, string, rubbers, rulers, pencils and little notebooks. There were colouring books, join-the-dot books, tracing books and those to which you applied your wet paintbrush and the colours appeared like magic. There were dolls in packets like little baby wetting dolls complete with bottle, little black dolls with earrings and red skirts, young lady dolls with handbags over their wrists and always of great interest to us, a tray of rings.

We kids had learned the best times to tackle Dad for pocket money and were usually successful when Mo was home, as he found it quite difficult to refuse her anything. Nevertheless, we knew better than to interrupt him when he was eating, so would hang around the back yard ready to ambush him when he'd finished his meal.

'Rings they wants, Lizzie!' he'd exclaimed one lunchtime when we'd told him what the money was for. 'Ye can have one through your noses if ye like and dat's all. My mate! Rings! Mudder o' God!'

All the same, he'd rattled his pocket and out of his work-blistered paw we had each picked out a sixpence from amongst a selection of screws, wingnuts, washers and half a tube of Polos.

'Ye has me skint, the lot o' ye,' he'd said mounting his bike and burping his way up the alley.

Mr Henry would allow me to take the ring tray outside to Mo. She would usually settle on a red one and I'd have an emerald green or pale blue. Any money left over would go on chews or a new notebook for 'Following,' a detective game we often played on unsuspecting individuals.

One afternoon Mum had sent us to check on Will who was fishing with Mick round Sevington.

'He doesn't see the danger,' she'd said.

There was nothing really dangerous about Sevington on a sunny afternoon back then before the age of the paedophile, but ever since he got lost at the seaside when he was three, Mum was always a little uneasy if Will wasn't visible out the front of the house.

The day he disappeared in Folkestone, Will and I had been building sandcastles minutes before. Mum had dozed off in a deck chair and woke to find only me on the sand. Hysterical, she dragged me through the crowds calling Will's name and asking people if they'd seen a little boy. With the beach covered in little boys and not one of them Will, the nightmare grew by the second. Mum began to whimper and I could not speak because of the huge lump of fear in my throat. Eventually we found Will at the Red Cross station clutching a nurse's hand looking relatively unmoved.

In Sevington he appeared quite safe, standing with Mick, knee-deep in the sparkling river. On the bridge sticklebacks flashed about in a jam jar. I held it up so that Mo could dip her fingers in and touch them. Under the echoing bridge were the shadows of two jug-eared boys and then me as I paddled towards them, my short bobbed hair giving the impression of a toadstool. Mo had got out of the chair and stood watching from the bridge. She liked to do this whenever she could as it made her feel as able-bodied as the rest of us, even if only for a little while. It was the sort of childhood scene on which you want to press the 'hold' button, but of course it slipped away as quickly as the sticklebacks around our feet.

Secret Agents

The area Patty and I called 'The Tree' was separated from the churchyard by a low wall. It had a pond in its centre, the surface of which resembled a pale green carpet. If a frog poked its head through momentarily, or we tossed in a pebble, the tiny green leaves would quickly re-form as though nothing had happened to disturb them. With the sun shining through the trees in summer, the place was Robin Hood's camp to us; in winter the Snow Queen's garden. There were several small pathways leading to what we called our 'lookout points.' A prickly yew tree would cover us completely if we climbed high enough into its middle. It was here that we first sampled the taste of a cigarette and then made a habit of picking up butts and lighting them. It was only when we started to feel ill that we realised this probably wasn't a good idea.

'Herbert,' the tree struck by lightening, was very easy to shin up, although the rear climber was always in danger of being clobbered by the occasional branch dislodged by the one in front.

I would point this all out to Mo from the lane as we returned from the Post Office or a walk around to Sevington Church. At the base of an elaborate memorial cross opposite the church door was a stone with the single word 'Entrance' etched upon it. I liked to think that this stone marked the opening to a secret tunnel from the church to the pub over the road, which was once an old cottage.

'It was how King Charles escaped from the Roundheads,' I would say knowledgeably, feeling sure that the King had spent most of his time hiding out around Willesborough. However, Mo didn't have much faith in my theories.

'I bet there isn't a tunnel,' she'd say. 'It's all made up, just a story.'

Nevertheless I would have entered the words, 'Tunnel' and 'Roundheads' in the notebook.

Our 'Following' game meant tailing some poor unsuspecting

individual as they went about their business. We would invent all kinds of intrigue around a simple trip to the shops or the barber's as had been the case with Mr Clough who worked with Dad in the factory. He had a very fast walk so we'd had our work cut out in following him.

Having seen Mr Clough approaching one day, we had stationed ourselves in the garages down the road in order to overtake him. Mo's chair had given us away as it had stuck out a bit. When Mr Clough had asked us if we were alright, we'd answered 'Yes, thank you,' huddled as we were between two garage walls. He'd smiled, obviously thinking we were quite mad, and then continued on with one hand behind his back as usual.

'That'd be the army,' said Mum when we'd reported back about Mr Clough's arm always being thus.

We had hurried out of the garages in time to see Mr Clough turn into the barber's. The note would have been something like 'Mr Cluff – haircut Saturday morning, hand behind back.'

Another time Mr Evans was our subject. He proved an altogether safer bet for tailing as he tended to plod rather than march like Mr Clough.

'He's going up the cemetery,' Mo had said when we'd spied Mr Evans heading up Mill View into Osborne Road.

Peeping through the hedge, we saw Mr Evans standing by 'Cariad' and thought it odd that he hadn't bothered with a watering can but was just gazing down at the white marble stone. We sensed that we shouldn't be spying but found it hard to move away and continued to squint through the hedge at Mr Evans in his shirtsleeves, his jacket hanging from his hand, brushing the grass.

We'd hung back a few yards until Mr Evans had turned out of the gate and made his way down the overhung path, his shoulders slightly hunched; his walk a little unsteady.

A couple of years had passed since David's demise and having no conception of the extent to which Mr Evans was still grieving, I noted down something like 'Mr Evans stood by Cariad for three minutes not moving. Then he put his hand over his eyes like he had a headache and then he went home.'

My fascination with 'mysteries' and my addiction to 'The Man From Uncle' often resulted in us playing the characters from the show.

I would play 'Ilya Kuryakin', Will was 'Napoleon Solo' and Mo got stuck with 'Mr Waverley.'

'Well, it makes sense really because he doesn't do much running about,' I explained. Needless to say, Mo wasn't too impressed and would often have lost interest and gone indoors by the time we came back to report some less than thrilling incident.

On one occasion, Will and I borrowed Dad's binoculars from his bedroom cupboard and, by crawling through the long grass down by the swings, followed the long suffering Mr Clough's progress to the chip shop. Will was then despatched to see what Mr Clough was ordering for his tea with instructions to report back to me where I'd be waiting in the 'sand bumps'. These were piles of sandy soil that had been dug out for the building of playground across the field years before but, never having been cleared away, grass had grown over them and they made brilliant hidey holes.

Through the binoculars, I eventually saw Mr Clough passing back along the road with his supper tucked under his arm. A few minutes later, Will appeared with the remains of a bag of chips.

'Mr Clough gave them to me,' he said. 'He saw me watching him through the window and he came out and asked me if I was hungry, so I said yes.'

There was hell to pay when Dad found out. He accused us of being no better than pikeys begging and bumming off of people and that we had put him to shame and no mistake. As usual, I got the brunt of his ire being the eldest and hadn't even had so much as a chip for my trouble either.

Undeterred, I started a secret club called 'The Red Star Agency,' the members of which were myself, Mo, Will, Mick and Patty. I made everyone a little book with a red star on the front and their agent number inside. I decided we were to meet in our shed every night at six and report what we had seen that was 'mysterious' during the day. All anticipation on the first evening, I set up some makeshift seats and waited. I knew Mo would be a bit late as she was having her hair washed over the sink. Patty duly showed up and reported having followed a man up to the Post Office where she had pretended to buy some chews while he'd gone into Mr Henry, 'as she had suspected,' for his pension money. Patty had then 'tailed' him through the cemetery where he'd sat down on the seat near the water cans and rolled a cigarette. He'd sat there for ages, she said and in the end she'd had to give up and go home as her mum had done her favourite for tea—egg and chips.

Mo came in eventually but only to avoid Mum's 'brushing up' of her hair. She said she hadn't seen much really but that sometimes people behaved suspiciously at Chailey and she would try and remember to write it down. After that we kept waiting for Will and Mick until Mum came out and asked us what we were all up to in the shed with the door shut. When I explained about our new club and that we were waiting for Will and Mick she laughed and said they'd gone out in the lorry with Dad ages ago.

The next evening they appeared but only to chuck their membership books down and announce they were leaving as clubs were for girls. Mo said she wanted to watch something on telly and Patty's dad turned up in search of her. I was left alone with five carefully made name badges and a sense of being somewhat alone in my imaginings.

That's Entertainment

The fascination to play at being someone else went far beyond childhood games with me. I really did want to be someone else, and not just one person either but several. I suppose for better or worse (it turned out to be worse), it was an early desire to act. Long after any of the TV dramas had finished, I was still thinking about the character and would often imagine myself in various roles. My favourite heroines at the time were 'Jane Eyre' and 'Katy Carr', who was played by Susan Hampshire in the TV series. I tried to copy her hairstyle with difficulty, mine being several inches shorter than hers.

Our first television set had arrived shortly after we moved house. It came in an enormous box with the letters GEC on the side. I found the box equally as interesting as the television itself as I could climb inside it and sitting alone in the dark imagine myself a parcel being posted all over the world.

One of the first programmes that I remember was a puppet show called 'Four Feather Falls'. This was followed a year or two later by the slightly more sophisticated 'Stingray' and 'Fireball XL5'. We had 'Noddy' and 'Twizzell' with his cat 'Footso'. Their friend, 'Jiffy the Broomstick Man' I always felt was a rather sinister character. All too often he would emerge from the chimney corner where he had been lurking as a harmless broom and threaten in a terrifying screech to 'Shake his twigs!'

There were American shows such as 'Life with the Lyons', 'William Bendix', 'Sergeant Bilko' and 'I Love Lucy'. As I got older, I thought it was great that Lucy and Desi Arnez were married in real life as well as in the show and really loved it when Lucy laughed or burst into tears. It was funny to see a grown woman behaving like a child with her enormous eyes and trembling lip.

Mum used to hoot at 'The Larkins' with Peggy Mount and David Kossoff, while I adored 'The Rag Trade' and Miriam Karlin's whistle followed by 'Everybody Out!' whenever Mr Fenner, boss of 'Fenner Fashions' dared to cross swords with her as shop steward.

After the demise of the 'detective agency', I turned theatrical impresario and threw myself into putting on a summer show in Patty's back garden. Patty and I practised our acrobatics on my swing as much as we could, along with a routine on the ground which involved her balancing on my hands and knees. She would then let go with one hand and raise it up to encourage applause. Next, I would hold out my arm so that Patty could do a 'backbend' over it. For our grande finale we'd both turn into crabs and walk along before jumping up and doing the splits, our arms held up in a final flourish.

We charged a penny at the gate to come in and Mum provided a packet of 'Rich Tea' biscuits to go with Patty's mum's orange squash for refreshments. The mums, Patty's nan and Mrs Cherry were our audience. Patty's dad remained in his shed fixing his radios even though we slid his invitation under the door.

Before our acrobatic routine, Mo, who had a lovely voice, sang a song and then we did a play that I'd made up about two sisters; one was good and one was bad and stole their mother's money. I was the good sister, Patty the bad one and Mo was the mother.

We had practised our parts well, having gone over and over them. The play was a success. Our acrobatic performance finished the show and almost finished us in to the bargain. During the routine Patty was to climb onto the overhead bar and drop down dramatically, hanging by her knees while I sat on the swing. We would then clutch hands while I swung to and fro.

Everything went well to start with. I did a lot of posturing and pointing to the swing and the bar to prepare the audience for our dynamic act. The only thing missing was a drum roll. Events took a turn for the worse when Patty did her 'drop down.' Having rehearsed this on my swing, we hadn't allowed for the fact that it was a little taller than Patty's. I sat smiling out at the audience and holding up my hands in anticipation of Patty's imminent arrival. When her head hit mine with a bloodcurdling thump I saw stars and little birds circling to a whistling noise like on 'Tom and Jerry'.

'I shouldn't worry,' said Mum when Patty's mother looked anxious. 'Might knock a bit of sense into them.'

My smile had turned into a fixed grin of pain and Patty's eyes were completely crossed when I gazed into her face, inches from my own. However, troupers to the last, we knew the show had to go on and pretended nothing untoward had happened. Our 'crabs' were all over the place with Patty dazedly crawling off out the gate at one point. When we stood up to take our bows, we were wobbling about like a couple of drunks. Nevertheless, we felt a huge sense of achievement even though our foreheads were sore for a few days afterwards.

All Creatures

Home for the holidays was Enid's foster daughter, Hilary, a big boned girl whose features were so masculine that she was often mistaken for a young man. One afternoon, when a few of us were walking through the cornfield opposite the church, a labourer working on the new housing estate looked at Hilary suspiciously and asked where she got her 'bumpy jumpers' from.

'Same place as you get those bumpy trousers from,' retorted Hilary.

Enid's husband had left several years before. 'Probably because of the strain of it all,' Mum said. Hilary had grown in both voice and stature and was now 'a proper handful'. Mum felt that it was due to Hilary being brought up in care that she lied the way she did and, with no mum to slap her legs when she was little, it wasn't surprising she had never got out of the habit.

'It's too late with kids like that,' she said. 'By the time they get to foster homes the damage has been done, poor little buggers. You can't help but feel sorry.'

Mum said the only time 'that Hilary girl' was of any use at all was the day she helped get a new chest of drawers up our stairs. Dad was out so we were all pushing and shoving and manoeuvring ourselves around the staircase when Hilary turned up at the front door with Matey in tow to see what all the commotion was about. She had no qualms about wandering into people's houses whenever she felt like it, but on that occasion it had been to our advantage.

'Stand back,' she said and heaving the thing up onto her chest, took it upstairs without any bother at all.

I fell victim to Hilary's fibbing once when having been entrusted with the school's collection of silkworms for the holidays, I returned from a family trip out to find their carefully woven cocoon missing from the cage.

Following a tip-off from Patty that she had seen her coming out of our gate clutching something in her hand, I challenged Hilary who swore blind that she knew nothing about it, even though, aside from Patty, she was the only one of our friends that I had shown it to. She said there was a girl up the road who liked cocoons and that it was more than likely her that had stolen it.

Shortly after that I decided that the silkworms might be pining either for their cocoon or the mulberry leaves that they fed on and which I could not produce as no such tree existed in the church yard or up the Broomies it seemed. Clearly, I had bitten off more than I could chew in taking them home, unlike the poor worms themselves who had nothing to bite on and even less to chew. Also, I decided they were extremely ugly and I wasn't sure whether I liked them or not after all. They must have been ravenous without the required leaves, so it seemed the kindest thing I could do was to bury them, the same way as Mum and I had done with a couple of gallons of her strawberry jam when, like the suitcase jellies, it had failed to set.

Mum dug the hole and I tipped the cage up so that the poor worms dropped in.

'I don't know why you took the poor things on in the first place,' said Mum. 'You know we don't have any luck with pets here.'

It was true. Apart from Joey the budgie who survived despite being poked at through the bars of his cage or ignored entirely for days, animals did not do well in our household. Joey's predecessor had flown out of the kitchen window when his cage door had been open for cleaning, never to be seen again. At Breadlands Road, my cat had caught distemper and died and my white hen, Sheila, disappeared one day without explanation. Goldfish fared quite badly too. Over the years several had been won at funfairs and been found floating on their sides after a few days, mainly due to starvation as we often forgot to feed them. One had suffered a particularly grisly end at the hands of Mo and Will when they decided to give it a ride on a toy train up and down the garden path. They were only small then and wondered why Freddie no longer moved when Mo prodded him with her finger as he lay staring in the driver's seat.

Later on, Will and I would catch little toads found under the pile of railway sleepers near the shed and race them in a bowl of water. We nicknamed them 'Burke' and 'Henry' after Gene Barry's character in

'Burke's Law' and 'Henry', his chauffeur. Luckily, the toads were none the worse for hours of being made to swim up and down whether they felt like it or not.

Then there were the slug executions. I couldn't stand slugs so I would sit up on the shed roof as Queen Cleopatra while Will, the Lord High Executioner placed each 'prisoner' on the chopping block.

'Slug,' I would say. 'You have been found guilty of being very ugly and making slime on the path. How do you plead?' (Courtroom terminology all got from 'Perry Mason'). There being no apparent response I would raise my arm and Will would raise the axe. When I gave the 'arm down' signal the slug would be despatched east and west, north and south like William Wallace, who I prefer to think, despite having no proof whatsoever from my researches into the family tree, may have been an ancestor of ours.

If in attendance, Mo would simply nod her head as the signal for the Lord High Executioner to bring down his axe. Three were despatched together one day when she had only been scratching her nose.

The last pet we had was a little black rabbit that ended up turning rogue due to lack of attention. As usual, he was a novelty start with, then Will and I lost interest and it was left to Mum to clean out his hutch. One day however, she put her foot down and told me to go and get on with it. I did my best to replace his dirty straw with fresh and while I was doing so, he managed to pee all over me. Goodness knows how he did it, but he angled his rear end and released all his pent-up rebellion in my general direction.

Needless to say, I had to report the 'loss' of the silkworms. Mum penned an apologetic note to 'Miss', in charge of class Three, explaining that they had not survived due to a shortage of the correct leaves. Luckily, Miss had forgotten all about them.

'We'll say no more about it,' she said goodnaturedly. 'But perhaps someone else should take the hamster at Christmas.'

The Baths, the Broomies and Holiday's End

The dusty two mile walk to Ashford swimming baths was always worth it on a hot afternoon, even though there wasn't much space in the water once you got there. The queue to get in snaked down the pavement and fights would break out as kids came face to face with those getting in before them.

The sign at the pay window gave the water temperature, which would then be passed along the queue, adding to the excitement of imminently getting in. The pool would be visible on this last lap – beautiful turquoise water with yellow ladders leading down into it at various intervals. Once through the turnstile you took a numbered band to a doorway where the pool man's wife handed you a basket for your clothes. Then it was off to the little wooden changing huts with the reflection of the water dancing off the walls. On any afternoon in the summer holidays the noise was deafening with kids repeatedly jumping in off the sides. The best you could hope for was to be able to 'dive for the bar' without someone landing on top of you.

Kids lay stretched out on the parched grass and what passed for a sun deck, the roof of a boiler house at the far end of the pool. Patrick was often among them. Patrick lived down near the swings. His house was dark and horrible inside if you looked through the window which we often did out of curiosity. Patrick's mother and father were really old and went down the club most nights. Once, when some boys beat him up, Patrick's jumper was pulled off to reveal a less than clean vest underneath. None of this seemed to affect Patrick's zest for life though and if he spotted us at the pool he would wave delightedly, a grey rag of a towel wrapped round his scorched, bony frame.

How different the pool was on our school visits with Miss! There would be only a dozen of us to disturb the glassy surface of the pool when we lowered ourselves in. When each one took a turn to jump, you could hear every detail of the splash it made on the surface, first the big splash itself and then all the little splashes that followed hissing away into nothing. 'Swimmers' were always allowed to go first in the dinner line as it was assumed we were hungrier than anybody else. During the holiday visits, Will and I would spend our bus fare home on sweets as we would always be ravenous. If we walked home with friends around the boards we knew better than to call in on Nana Spice, as to turn up with a 'regiment' meant a shooing off from behind the kitchen curtain. We often looked in on our 'tree house' beside the river. This tree when covered in blossom, was spread out like a beautiful umbrella. Sitting beneath its shade we could not be seen from the main road which made it all the more our 'secret place'.

We often walked to the Broomfields to slide down the sandy banks and play on rope swings, our voices echoing through the overhanging trees. Across the road from here was the house where Nana Spice was born in 1903 to Frank and Louisa. It was then called 'Number One Sandybank' and, according to Uncle Bernard, had a well in the garden. I like to think of Nan as 'Ellen', a little girl running through those woods in a white smock all excited at her Dad's imminent arrival home on leave for he was then still in the 'Rifles'. A few yards down the road was Willesborough hospital where Mo and I were born and where Nana Spice would sadly pass away in 1974; her life having begun and finished within two hundred yards of the same stretch of road.

The summer holidays would roll on with one day running into the next and nothing more for us to think about than which game to play. Then all too soon it was time to visit 'Armstrongs', the local outfitters for those items of school kit that could not be stretched to another year. The place smelled of starched cotton and old style efficiency. It was run like a battleship by Mr Armstrong, a spare man with sticky out ears and a lisp. A loud clang from the doorbell would announce our arrival and was usually the cue for Mr Armstrong's assistant, Mrs Thwaite to become extremely busy, dusting off the counter or dressing the half torso that stood at one end of it, thereby avoiding having to deal with us. Mrs Thwaite, with her black bouffant hairstyle and swooping glasses, resembled a character from a 'Larson' cartoon. Her ideal customers would be those females who loved to gossip and with whom she could impress with tales of her only daughter, Letitia who as I once earwigged lived on the 'Ale of Wate'.

To Mr Armstrong, the clang of the doorbell meant the clang of the till so he would leap eagerly forward to Mum's assistance.

'Hold your armth out, Thunny Jim,' he'd say applying his tape measure to Will. 'Hmmm. Now thit down on the thtool and let me methur your foot for thooth. Goodneth me. You're growing at the rate of knotth.'

Dear Mr Armstrong would climb up his push-along steps in search of shoes and then crawl along the floor Cossack-style, pulling open drawers of shirts. The top of his head moving along behind the counter would set us sniggering.

When all purchases had been made, Mr Armstrong would place Mum's cash in a tiny capsule and launch it on a wire across the room to where the owl-like Miss Cole, keeper of the shop ledger, sat in her glass fronted pulpit. Their exchange would go something like this:

'Enter Mith Cole.'

'Yes, Mr Armstrong.'

'One boy'th thcool thirt, theven and thixth.'

'One boy's school shirt, seven and six.'

'One pair boy'th thcool thoooth, fifteen thillingth.'

'One pair of school shoes, fifteen shillings.'

'Thatth all, thank you, Mith Cole.'

Mr Armstrong would then deftly parcel up our goods in brown paper, tie the string with a flourish, and snip off the loose ends with a pair of enormous scissors, before seeing us to the door with a farewell salute and a 'Much obliged.'

I invariably had new shoes for the autumn term but, aside from my toes pinching as I set off to school, I would have an uncomfortable feeling in my throat like I'd swallowed a sharp-ended chip. This was due to the imminent arrival of a man from the Social Services who would escort Mo out of the front door and down the path to his car. The thought of this would be with me all day until I returned home to find Mum red-eyed and jumpy. We would all watch TV in the evening without saying much and at bedtime I would lay down without Mo to chat to and without Dad's usual repartee as he passed by the door.

The prospect of Mo's departure always hung over us throughout the previous day like an oppressive cloud. However, Mo's sense of humour stood her in good stead for even then she would find something amusing to say. I remember on one occasion we'd been up to the Post Office for a last look at the ring tray and were making our way between the graves gazing at our shadows on the path.

'Look,' said Mo, who'd had her hair trimmed at Carola's. 'I look like Joey with this haircut.'

Sure enough when she moved her head quickly back and forth her shadow did indeed resemble our budgie nodding at himself in his mirror. I screeched out laughing.

'No, thanks. I want Trill!' she said as I handed her a 'Penny Arrow.'

Mo may have compared herself to a budgerigar, but on those awful mornings in the square, she was as brave as a lion.

My Little Grey School

Being in Class Three was a great relief after Class Two where everything awful seemed to happen to me. The teacher there had been very strict and would yell at us from behind her desk throughout the day. Not having a particularly loud voice, she often resorted to hurling missiles to gain our attention. These ranged from the blackboard eraser to one of a selection of rulers she kept in her desk for the purpose. She leaned to one side when she walked, probably from years of carrying a huge leather bag full of class work. To have to stand before her was something I dreaded and I would avoid doing so wherever possible. Rather than

My Little Grey School

ask for help if I was stuck during arithmetic, I would make myself more conspicuous by sitting for the whole lesson at my desk just staring at my sum book. Teacher would then haul me out and explain the sum as if it was the easiest thing in the world, while I concentrated on her mouth which was a cavern of uneven teeth.

'Got it?' she would ask.

'Oh, yes, thank you,' I would answer, sloping back to my desk none the wiser.

I had sat next to a boy called Michael who had breath like baked beans, a laugh like a seal and a habit of wiping the desk over with his sleeve. One morning he'd turned up sporting a brand new red jumper, the sleeve of the old one having done overtime the previous day when he'd pressed too hard on his bottle top spraying milk everywhere. Michael smelled clean in the new jumper and not too beany for once, so having decided he might be a safe bet as a future partner, I asked if he'd like to marry me.

What possessed me to think that an eight year old boy would keep something like that a secret, I really don't know – probably because I was eight myself at the time. Not surprisingly, Michael began laughing at full seal.

'Oi, you lot, guess what she's just said?' he yelled out.

'Please don't! Please!' I begged, clinging to that now treacherous jumper, but there was to be no reprieve. The whole class was in hysterics by the time teacher entered the room clutching the school wireless half her size.

'What on earth's going on?' she asked, depositing the wireless on the desk and reaching for the blackboard eraser to hurl at no-one in particular.

My face turned scarlet as Michael explained, repeating my proposal yet again. As teacher shook her head in despair, I turned to the shiny green wall praying for a passing train to de-rail at the foot of the playground and come crashing right through. No such luck though. It took several days to live that incident down, during which time Michael became more 'beany' and 'sealy' than ever.

Father Joe, the Parish Priest, sometimes visited us during 'Jigsaw time' on Friday mornings. We would have to break off from whichever puzzles were working on, usually either 'Maps of the World' or 'Holy

67

Pictures,' to stand up for a blessing. I always had an uneasy suspicion that whatever I said in the confessional might cause Father Joe to break his vows and pass my misdemeanors on to Teacher, who I felt didn't need much convincing that I was a hopeless case. One morning when I was in the middle of piecing together 'China and Japan', I fancied I saw them whispering together and looking in my direction. From then on I rarely said much at all when I knelt down on the spongy matting in the dark confessional box at the back of the church, even though I knew I ran the risk of going to hell by keeping any sins to myself. In hell I imagined you got branded like on 'Rawhide' or poked like those sausages that sizzled in the pan on the advert and that the branding and poking never stopped but went on forever.

I mentioned my fears of hell to Mum once and she said not to worry, it was probably an old wives' tale like putting a stocking round your throat if it was sore, or using the 'paper bag' cure for a wart. When I asked her to expand on the 'paper bag' theory she explained that if you put a stone in a paper bag and throw it away where you would never see it again the wart was supposed to disappear along with it. I tried this many times hoping to remove the blight on my wedding finger. Several bagged up stones went in the dustbin, into the river at Sevington and once onto the top of a train as it passed beneath the railway bridge, but still the wart remained.

The incident with Michael had left me dreading any kind of attention being drawn to myself at school. Therefore, I was horrified one morning when on rising from the toilet my knickers fell to the ground, the elastic having given out. For the remainder of the day, I kept my arm firmly pressed against my body to prevent my drawers slipping down to my ankles. At playtimes I managed by standing against the wall but lunchtime was a huge feat of accomplishment as I balanced my plate in one hand. I remember being in a right old tizzy by the time I got home.

'What on earth's the matter?' asked Mum. I finally let go and my knickers fell to the floor. Despite my day of endurance, I burst out laughing with relief as Mum deposited the useless articles into the dustbin.

'Why didn't you ask teacher for a pin?' she asked. Mum always had safety pins at the ready for every eventuality. I would rather have stuck pins in my eyes than ask Teacher for one. Added to which, to get the pin open and closed again each time I needed the loo might have proved a little difficult. I would have probably have ended up stabbing myself into the bargain and still tried to keep that a secret.

One of the few lessons I had enjoyed in Class Two was singing along to the big wireless. This was probably because we could sing as loud as we wanted. I would join in with the story of 'The Merry Cobbler' for all I was worth. One day I decided to treat Mum and Dad to a rendition using the front room hearth as a stage. Gazing up at the ceiling, I'd sung at the top of my voice:

'A Merry Cobbler man am I, fah lah dah dee rah!
I sit and mend as days go by,
Fah lah dah dee rah dee,
Fah lah dah dee rah!'

When I'd finished I saw to my horror that they were doubled up with laughter. I ran upstairs and threw myself wailing on the bed like Scarlett O'Hara, listening desperately for the creak of a stair. When none came, I got up and put a few things in my plimsoll bag, probably something like a pencil, a notebook and a bottle of diluted orange, went downstairs and headed out the back door. 'They'll be sorry,' I thought to myself. Mum and Dad were having a cup of tea at the table and didn't seem to notice my departure.

Halfway to the station I realised that having no money might pose a bit of a problem. I called in on Nan who gently talked me out of departing for London and walked half the way back with me. She said she understood how I was feeling but assured me that even though my parents had laughed at my 'performance' I was loved a great deal. It was difficult to see that back then of course.

I was chosen as one of the singers in the Christmas concert that year and Teacher told us to watch carefully one afternoon while she demonstrated how to make the crowns we would be wearing for the event.

'I'm only going to tell you once,' she emphasized.

We had to colour the paper first with a Christmas scene of our choice and then fold and cut it 'like so.' Teacher opened her crown up into a row of even little points. Of course, when I opened mine it fell apart. I quickly gathered the paper shards up from the desk but not before Teacher had spotted me. Out to the front of class I had to go.

'This is how you don't do it,' said Teacher, dropping paper bits all over my head while everyone guffawed.

When I told Mum of my 'coronation' she immediately came to the rescue by removing the bottom of an old shoe box and turning its sides into a crown to fit my head. Then mixing up some flour and water paste she covered the whole thing in bright red and black Christmas paper, embossed with touches of glitter here and there. After topping it off with a strand of tinsel, she presented me with what I felt was the most magical crown ever made. As it was totally different from everyone else's, Teacher had no option next day but to place me centre stage for the event. Beaming out at Mum as Anne wriggled on her lap and Teacher plonked away on the piano to 'Away In A Manger,' I felt like a queen for the afternoon.

My new classroom, Class Three, was tucked away around the side of the school building, its lobby door opening onto the 'big boy's' playground and the kitchen beyond. Throughout the morning the cooks' banter and the clatter of pans rang out of its open windows on great puffs of steam.

Each classroom in this quaint little building with its gothic shaped doors and windows was equipped with a black stove surrounded by a brass topped fireguard. It was around this that we would huddle on frosty mornings, chilblains itching in our damp shoes.

Along the walls ran a frieze of the Blessed Sacraments. Most interesting to me were 'Matrimony' and 'Extreme Unction' as marriage and death were the subjects that I found most significant in life at that time, what with pursuing Rupert and hanging around churchyards the way I did. However, the picture of 'Matrimony' looked rather gloomy compared to Rose's wedding. The bride and groom standing before a grim faced priest looked as if they were about to be led to the gallows rather than start their married life.

In 'Extreme Unction' a priest prayed over a dying old man while a dove hovered at the window. It made death look quite a straightforward and peaceful experience.

I did well in Class Three as my new teacher, or 'Miss' specialised in those pursuits that I enjoyed the most, like country dancing and story writing. One morning she set us a composition to write our earliest memories. I probably wrote about the Christmas I found Susie, my black doll, in a box under the sideboard but looking back now my first real memory was of a summer evening in 1957.

I was walking through a field with Dad and Mo. All around was golden light. Dad was celebrating something. It could have been the birth of Will, a son at last, or the fact that the local Council had granted us a larger house, or knowing Dad, just life in general. In any case, his laughter was infectious as he bounced Mo on his shoulders, even though her hands wouldn't have responded when he squeezed them and she wouldn't have been able to reach out to Mum when we got home. I brought up the rear, pushing knee deep through the long grass, trying to keep in Dad's shadow and catch some of his joy. As he reached the stile at end of the field, he turned towards me with a smile and held out his hand. It was the beginning of life as I remember it.

Miss had a pink cardigan similar to one owned by Nana Spice and similar wavy grey hair. She seemed very old to me, as did all my teachers, but was probably only in her late forties. On rainy days, she wore a blue mac with a matching hat and if she saw Will and I making our way around the boards in the rain with autumn leaves blowing in our faces, she would stop her little Morris Minor car with the tiny statue of Our Lady on the dashboard and pick us up, even though our shoes might be muddy and our macs soaking wet.

On fine days or even cold ones if it wasn't raining, Miss would get us, the members of her form, to do exercises in the playground. We'd copy her in running on the spot, twisting from the waist and leaping into star shapes. One windy day, as she performed the exercise of raising one leg and passing it through her joined hands, I caught a fleeting glimpse of long pink bloomers. I found this rather disconcerting as to my way of thinking, teachers weren't meant to be like other ladies and did not have underwear or go to the toilet. Beneath their skirts I imagined they had a petticoat that was stitched on and their lower halves were like dolls, plain pink and sexless.

Miss sometimes brought in roses to place over the fireplace beneath a picture of St Teresa of Avila. It was the rose bushes in the front garden and the Morris Minor with Our Lady on the dash that gave away which one in the row of houses near the railway crossing was hers when I decided to seek it out one evening.

I stood at the gate imagining Miss sitting behind the net curtains, marking exercise books and chatting to 'Mrs Ramsay' with whom she shared the house. She often referred to Mrs Ramsay in conversations with other teachers which I earwigged in passing, or when I deliberately loitered nearby to do up my shoelace.

'Yes,' she'd say. 'I wholeheartedly agree. I was only discussing this with Mrs Ramsay last evening' or 'Oh, yes. Quite. Mrs Ramsay is of the same opinion as a matter of fact.'

I'd often wondered what Mrs Ramsay looked like and tried to put together a photofit in my head as I stood gazing at the house beyond the roses. She was small and quite delicate I decided, that's why she didn't go out much, but only pottered about until Miss came home. She wore a lot of lacy dresses and her name would of course be Rose whereas Miss, I imagined, had been christened something 'no-nonsense', like Maude or Gertrude.

A new term invariably meant new books with fresh pages crackling as you turned them. We were handed pristine copies of 'Early Britain,' but it didn't take long for the Picts and Scots or King Canute to become soiled by grubby fingers. We were taking it in turns to read one day when I became preoccupied with how long it would take to grow my hair like 'Rowena,' the wife of a chieftain, if for once Mum would spare me from Alison's scissors *('Just below the ears, please')*. When it was my turn to read I found I was completely lost. The boy next to me came to the rescue and pointed out the place on the page. His finger, grubby though it may have been, at least knew where to find Hadrian's Wall.

As autumn leaves whirled about the yard and stuck to the windows, Miss set us the task of writing about them. You had to go outside, find one that you liked the shape of and write a story about it. I found my composition book in an old wooden chest years later when I was in my teens. I'd written something along the lines of there being loads of brown and yellow leaves at the bottom of the 'magic' tree by the gate and that when I put my arms around that tree it was like a big man and smelled wet and green stuff got under your nails if you scratched it. I went on about leaves following you along the road and blowing about like they couldn't care less, that if you pulled a leaf apart when it was young and green you'd find its 'skellinton' underneath and leaves stuck to your shoes so that your mum told you off when you brought them indoors.

Miss tried to make our geography lesson as interesting as possible with the help of 'Mother Owl' stories. These were slightly more compelling than the Picts and Scots as they involved a boy and an owl travelling the world together. The boy would be awakened late at night by Mother Owl tapping on the window with her beak. He would then climb onto her back and away they'd fly to another land. They had a different adventure each night in places such as Tibet, 'the Roof of the World' or Japan, 'Land of the Midnight Sun.' Once they went to the desert and an Arab showed the boy how to survive a sandstorm by snuggling up to his camel and pulling his robes over his head.

I was always well behaved at school, mainly through fear of authority. The teachers aside, I knew Dad was very keen for me to do well. I tried hard once I'd settled down into the routine, but like many I had found my first morning to be nothing short of a nightmare. There was no 'playschool' then of course, no gentle lead up to being parted from your mother for a couple of hours a day to get you gradually used to the idea. Primary school was full on severance and horror. Mum had done her best to pave the way, explaining that it was only for a little while and there'd be lots of other boys and girls to play with. But I couldn't get over her treachery at handing me to a complete stranger before disappearing in a whirl of her checked coat.

Dad in the factory (circa 1961)

73

Up until then, mine had been a cosy world of Victor Sylvester's music on the radio in the mornings and 'Watch With Mother' in the afternoons. I would get annoyed if Mum shirked her half of the bargain and took a nap during 'Picture Book' or 'Andy Pandy', let alone abandon me for hours on end in a class full of noisy strangers.

The mistress of the infants' class had told us to put our hands up if we wanted to be excused. A boy put his hand up and said he wanted to go home but Miss said that was rather silly and you only put your hand up if you needed to go to the toilet. It was all very nerve-wracking. Dad had warned that if I didn't behave at school, there'd be a big stick to sort me out. I was therefore quite relieved to find that the stick which stood in the corner of the classroom was used for nothing more than opening the tall windows.

Behind the teacher's desk in that first little classroom was a cupboard full of books, boxes of chalk, and tubs of a wonderful white glue paste called 'Gripfix'. This had to be applied with a spatula and its marzipan smell was quite hypnotic. No doubt this has long been discontinued due to possible 'glue sniffing' problems, although in my case it was more a question of glue 'nibbling' so attractive did I find it. On the walls were pictures of rabbits and over the mantelpiece a rather macabre print of the face of Our Lord wearing the crown of thorns. His eyes would open and close in a 3D effect depending on the angle from which you looked at the print. The room smelled strongly of wood, chalk, coal dust from the railway and general strangeness.

Janet, with whom I shared a desk, loved to dance and at playtimes we would do 'Round the World'. This involved twirling each other around and humming the Nat King Cole song or what I could remember of it from the radio. The idea was to get our skirts billowing out as far as possible like ladies' dresses when they did the Jive down the club.

Simone would get 'Potato Puffs' or 'Jammy Dodgers' from the tuck shop at playtime while I nibbled at a marmalade sandwich. However, I soon accepted that the tuck shop was a luxury Mum couldn't afford and stopped yearning for its contents. Besides, bringing money to school and finding it again for 'tuck' would have been quite an undertaking for me back then. You knew where you were with a marmalade sandwich, even if it was quite misshapen after being squashed in your satchel all morning.

Dad would meet me at lunchtimes until I settled down. Steering his pushbike with his large brown hands either side of my own, he'd peddle around the boards with me on the crossbar. The trouble was I never wanted to return for the afternoon session and would sit staring through the gothic windows at the blue sky, listening to the banging and hammering from the factory next door, wondering which noise my dad was making. When he was six years old, Dad received a certificate for not missing one day at school and was always stressing the importance of education.

Of course, as the days went on, the noise faded into the background and I noticed it less and less as I became more interested in what was taking place in school. At twelve o'clock I was no longer waiting for Dad at the gate, but lining up with my plate for a 'big one' of whatever was on the menu.

Grace was said before lunch and prayers between each lesson. As soon as 'Bless us, oh Lord, for these thy gifts which we are going to receive through thy bounty, through Christ, Our Lord. Amen' was uttered, and the signal given from whichever teacher was supervising, we would grab a plate and fall in line. The dinner ladies in their green overalls would load us up with roast or stew and vegetables followed by 'Banana Custard', 'Gypsy Tart' or 'Chocolate Popcorn' with syrup. Friday fayre was usually fishcakes, salad and cheesy mashed potato. There was much consternation one Friday when slices of bread replaced mash due to a shortage of potato supplies to the school. On rare afternoons, left over sponge pudding would be trayed around the playground to packs of baying wolves, myself among them.

As I remember, mornings in the infant class were spent copying down numbers, doing simple little sums or mixing paint from the large tins on the table. As with Gripfix, I found the smell of the brightly coloured powder intoxicating. Sometimes we'd cut out paper shapes with round ended scissors or take crayons from an old brown box and draw 'ladies and mans.'

The afternoons would end with a song such as 'My Little Grey Donkey' ('would trot to the fair') or a story into which I would always feel myself drawn. Then a whistle would be blown and it was out to the gate where Mum stood waving beneath the trees.

'Janet and John' figured greatly in our reading lessons and I was fascinated, not only by their adventures with kites and toy aeroplanes, but also by the colours used to portray them. We then progressed to Aesop's Fables; I loved the story of 'The Hare and the Tortoise' and also the 'Sun and the Wind' when they competed at getting a man to take his coat off.

CORK SCHOOL ATTENDANCE COMMITTEE

◆

Certificate of Merit

This is to Certify that

Liam Ó Súilleabáin

of *4 St. Mary's Avenue* has attended School

on every school day at *Cathedral N.* School

during the year ended the 31st day of December, 19*37*, and this

Certificate is awarded as a mark of appreciation by the Committee

of the Student's efforts to attain that efficiency which is only obtained

by constant application to *his* studies, and which is so essential to

the success of *his* career in whatever profession or occupation *he*

chooses to pursue.

Dated this *31ad* day of *Mí na Nodlaz* 193*7*.

Daniel Cohalan Chairman

————— Secretary

PARSONS, CORK

Dad's school attendance certificate, 1937 when he was six years old

Being in Class Three meant I was about half way through my primary education. I had been admitted a few weeks after my fifth birthday in August 1958, so was always one of the youngest in each class.

One morning the headmaster from the school next door put in an appearance at Assembly. This was a rarity as Mr Barnes only ever paid a visit to complain about boys throwing stones over the fence into his playgrounds or all of us making too much noise going out the gate at home time. However, on this occasion, he had a smile beneath his moustache as he stood beside our headmistress.

'Mr Barnes has a question,' she said, all smiles too which was also rare. Mr Barnes said 'Good morning' and proceeded to tell us about a trip to Dover Castle planned for the following day. There were two places left on the coach.

'Who would like to go?' asked the headmistress gazing out at a sea of raised arms, mine included. I'd been to Windsor Castle before and really enjoyed it so the idea rather appealed. I was delighted when she picked me, but not so happy when she chose a boy called Alec Smedley to be my travelling companion.

'We will meet you at the gate at a quarter to nine,' said Mr Barnes 'And don't be late.'

As the day wore on, the shine of the trip wore off. Alec was a rather unpopular sort of boy from quite a 'posh' family. He didn't think he ought to hurry for anything and was rarely seen running or taking part in any games that required much movement. He had once been found dozing during a story about 'Topsy The Angel'. Being a complete 'Topsy' fan myself, I had found this quite astonishing. At 'home time' Mr Smedley would sit waiting in an old Daimler until Alec deigned to make an appearance, dragging his feet and satchel. Mr Smedley would then perform a complicated three-point turn getting in the way of the school bus and clogging up the tiny road even more.

I wished that the likes of Helen, who enjoyed the occasional game of 'Cowgirls' was coming with me or even Janet for that matter who could turn me upside down like Margot Fonteyn on the 'Palladium'. I couldn't concentrate on lessons for worrying and got an ear bashing from Miss during arithmetic for not paying attention.

In the afternoon, during 'Early Britain,' I was so preoccupied that, when it was my turn to read, I started on about 'Hereward the Wake' when everyone else was on 'Boadicea in Battle.' Miss said she despaired.

When Mum met us at the gate I thought about telling her my predicament, but Anne was grizzling and had been a 'little mare' at Nan's apparently. It had come on to rain and the pram wheels were all stuck with leaves. Will, who had an upset tum, had been slow to put up his hand in class so that all Mum wanted to do was get home quickly as possible. As we walked around the boards I thought about running back with the excuse that I wasn't allowed to go, but school was scary after hours as I'd found out when I left Dad's fountain pen behind and had gone back for it. He had loaned the pen to me for 'joined up writing' on the strict understanding that I bring it home every night. The deserted classroom had been eerie with all the chairs placed on the desks in preparation for the cleaners, our final task after the end of day prayer. The ticking of the clock, barely noticeable when the room was full, had sounded really loud and I had felt the chairs themselves had eyes. What if Miss had already gone home and Mr Pick, the caretaker, locked me in by accident? I just hung onto the pram and wished I'd never stuck my bloomin' hand up in the first place.

The next morning I dawdled behind Will and Mick, loitering at the particular factory entrance where the men worked the steam hammer. I watched it sending out showers of sparks each time it fell. Hopefully, I reasoned, the bus would go without me and the whole episode just slip away. Further sparks were to fly though as the coach then appeared around the corner with Mr Barnes, seated up the front near the driver like a meerkat on full alert.

'Are you coming?' he shouted, leaning out of the door. Kids were gawping out of the windows including Alec Smedley, wide awake for once.

When I said 'no,' Mr Barnes shook his head in exasperation and went back inside. Needless to say, that wasn't the end of it. Half way through Assembly the headmistress realised that I was among the throng as usual and not on the way to Dover.

'Come here immediately,' she said, focusing on me like an eagle would its prey. Out I went to be chided in front of the whole school.

Up until that point, there had only been the usual notices about attending Mass on Sunday and a collection for the foreign missions so everyone was up for a spot of light entertainment.

'What on earth do you think you're playing at?' The headmistress's face was red and her chin a bit fluffy I noticed, close up. 'Do you realise how long Mr Barnes waited for you this morning?'

While she admonished me in this way, accusing me of letting both her and the entire school down, I tried to concentrate on the shiny whistle she always wore around her neck which that morning was set off sharply against her black sweater. I could just about make my face out in it – a mouse staring.

'Don't you realise someone else could have gone in your place?' the headmistress went on. What feeble answers I was trying to form would not allow themselves to be spoken. I looked along the line of teachers for

The 'Magic Tree' and the bead-swapping step

support from 'Miss', but even if she felt so inclined she was obviously not going to cross swords with the headmistress on my behalf. I thought of those pink bloomers and how she was just the same as everyone else underneath.

I sat alone at playtime for the rest of the day avoiding the stares of other kids. No-one wanted to be seen associating with me, a troublemaker who had wasted not only my own but someone else's chance of Dover Castle. During the afternoon break I took myself off into the 'big girl's' playground which overlooked one of the factory yards. Sometimes Dad could be spotted down there driving a fork lift truck. One afternoon he had abandoned it to retrieve long forgotten tennis balls from the long grass and had thrown them up to Will and myself. No such luck that day though, the yard was full of men working, but not one of them was Dad.

I was sitting on the step near the gate feeling sorry for myself when a girl I'd never seen before came and sat beside me. Lots of her straight, wispy hair had escaped from the stretchy band which had slipped to the back of her head. She was constantly rubbing her arm like it was second nature to do so.

'Want to swap beads?' she asked, the rubbing now having moved to her face.

'Ain't got none,' I said.

'You mean you haven't got any,' she corrected in a very nice voice. 'Can you bring some tomorrow and meet me here on the step?'

'Alright then,' I answered. 'Why do you keep scratching?'

'I've got excema.'

She pointed out the places where her skin was worst affected by little white scales. I slid my fingers along her arm and wanted to say 'ugh!' but did not, having realised after the morning's experiences how it felt to be an oddity. Meanwhile, Winnie, for that was her name, had produced a matchbox from her pocket. She pushed it open very carefully to reveal a beautiful purple glass stone nestling in a bed of cotton wool.

'It's my best one,' she said taking it out and holding it up to the light. 'Want to hold it?'

Through the bead, the lime trees in the yard turned purple, as did the sky, the school gate and the gardens over the road. The glass was multi-faceted and, in it, I saw that the fearful mouse expression reflected in the head's whistle earlier had turned into a hundred smiles.

Ellen Wallace (Nana Spice) in 1919 aged 16

Ellen and friend around the time she worked at the George Hotel

Mum aged 2

Me with Dairylea

Myself with Mum in 1954
(Not keen on
headgear even then, but
worse was to come)

Myself with
Nana Spice 1954
shortly after
Grandfather died

Uncle John could
make me smile

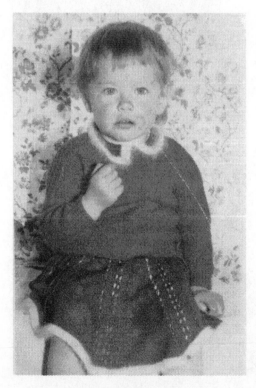

At Breadlands
Road 1955

Myself and Mo in 1957

Will, myself and a
neighbour around the
time he went AWOL
in Folkestone

At Twelve Acres in
1958 – (Note the
sneaky Bex Bissell
in the corner)

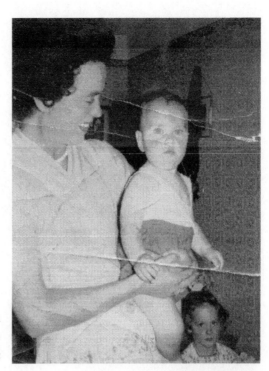

**Not happy with
Will hogging the
limelight**

El Bolero

Will, myself, Mo and Anne 1962

The Clocktower at the entrance to the railway works

Weekend at Nan's

Nana Spice's house was one of several little pebble-dashed homes situated a few hundred yards up the street from the factory. They were known as the 'gas houses' and had been built for the first railway workers. It was the promise of acquiring number 235 that had prompted Grandfather Spice to give up his job at the Kennington chalk pits. As it turned out, the move was ill-fated as his job in the railway involved working with asbestos-lined engines before its lethal effects were known. The Spices of Kennington were country people and had worked for generations on the land. Granddad found life at the factory difficult to adapt to; it wasn't in his blood, unlike asbestosis poisoning which would be after a few short years.

**Grandfather Spice (centre) with mates in the railway.
The work he undertook was to prove fatal**

Nan kept her garden as tidy as the house's interior. Forsythia crept over the wooden fence at the back and vibrant pink clover grew along foot of the outside wall along with bluebells in early summer. Nan was often to be found there turning earth over with a little fork and pulling out weeds, her skirt swinging to and fro with the effort. A walkway ran between her house and the one next door, banked either side by a picket fence. I once had my photograph taken there wearing my 'flowerpot' dress and a bolero that Nan had given me as a present. 'You look lovely in that bollyro,' she'd said. 'Let's have a snap.' The bolero was light blue with bunnies on. However, being made of something like tarpaulin it was pretty useless as an article of clothing, except maybe for Irish dancing where arms were never lifted and which I never did anyway. It wasn't long before it went the same way as my baggy knickers.

Opposite Nan's was a large, mysterious house set back behind trees. I was always peeping through the fence at the deserted driveway or trying the garden door's little bracelet handle to no avail. Nan said that parties were once held at the house when the people who had lived in it were young. I imagined ladies in flapper dresses arriving in shiny cars while Charleston music played in the house like in 'The Roaring Twenties' on TV. The roof and upper windows were visible from Nan's front bedroom window and, whenever I stayed overnight, this was the view I woke up to.

When I couldn't face the trip to Chailey in whatever mode of transport Dad had secured for the journey, I would stay with Nan; sometimes just for the day and occasionally overnight. One sunny morning Dad dropped me off at the end of Nan's road before setting off with Mum, Anne and Will in a Vauxhall Victor; its seats, being covered in a smelly plastic material, would have had me green in no time at all.

When I found Nan's back door closed, I got myself into a panic thinking she had forgotten I was coming and gone up town or worse still, to Uncle John's at Gravesend for the day. This was unlikely, I reasoned, for on such trips I was 'her ears' as she often said. I turned the handle and was relieved when the door opened.

The kitchen was quiet apart from tap's slow drip into the stone sink and there was the usual smell of Camay in the air. Nan would have been up early as always for her wash down. She was always washing her hands throughout the day, rubbing them hard with a pumice stone. Her preoccupation with cleanliness probably came from childhood days when, if she wasn't being scrubbed herself, she was scrubbing neighbours' clothes with her mother. This continued on as, for several years, she had worked in a laundry operating a press to keep other people's sheets neat. She would yank a comb, never a brush through her hair. When she ate a meal, she always washed up and put away quickly as though the meal and the pleasure of eating it had never been.

A newly washed yellow cup and saucer were drying on the wooden drainer and the kettle was warm. The patterned curtains were pulled back but the room was as dark as ever due to the high wooden fence outside. I was apprehensive – something wasn't quite right and I almost wished I had gone to Chailey after all. Perhaps the plastic smell wouldn't have been so bad with the window open if I'd taken a 'Kwell', but it was too late now. Nan had to be in the house somewhere. The trick was to find her before she found me as, if she wasn't wearing her hearing aid, she wouldn't appreciate my appearing unexpectedly out of the shadows and giving her 'heart failure'.

I became conscious of a vague sound coming from above. It sounded like coughing. Could Nan be ill? I moved into the hall and stood at the foot of the stairs wondering whether or not to call out. Again came the sound – a voice, a clearing of the throat. Slowly I began to ascend, one sandal at a time on the carpeted stair. Light exuded from the window in the small bedroom ahead. This was once my Mum's room where, as a child, she'd sat in bed with her books and sweets. It was really too small for the size of the bed it contained.

'It's a proper feather bed,' Nan always stressed. Uncle Bernard's wife, Auntie Lee, would tell me a few years later how she once shared this bed with Mum when the house was full.

'Oh well,' said Lee, who had been pregnant with my cousin Geoff at the time. 'It's big enough for the two of us - I mean the three of us!'

'The four of us as a matter of fact,' Mum had quipped betraying my embryonic existence. Geoff and I were born within a few days of each other in August 1953.

Nan's room was along the landing and faced out front. It was from here that the sound was coming. As I drew nearer it occurred to me that

Nan was not coughing but weeping. I reached the doorway and slowly peered around. Somewhere in the distance a steam engine shrieked a warning the way they always did on entering a tunnel. In the dressing table mirror I saw my grandmother seated on the bed, crying into a handkerchief and calling my grandfather's name.

I decided the best thing I could do was to make myself scarce, so I crept back down and hid in the under-stairs cupboard. There I stood with the door ajar, breathing in the coaly smell which had never quite disappeared even though none had been stored there for years. On the little shelf were a few handy items – a tin of plasters, some 'Three-in-One' oil, a sewing kit, but nothing to mend a broken heart.

It wasn't the first time I had seen Nan in tears. She had cried on saying goodbye to Uncle Bernard after he had visited from America the previous year with Auntie Lee and my cousins.

Having emigrated after a couple of years in Farnborough where he worked as an aeronautical engineer, Uncle Bernard had settled in Canada going from strength to strength in his career. By the time of the visit I speak of, he and his family had moved to the States and were living in Huntsville, Alabama.

They had been staying at a house in Kingston-Upon-Thames for part of their visit. Nan and I had spent the last few days with them. Uncle Bernard had hired a car and taken us to visit some historical places of interest; that was how I'd seen Windsor Castle. By the time we got to the castle I remember there was a big wet patch on the back of Uncle Bernard's shirt from the effort of driving in the heat.

I'd seldom spoken to Uncle Bernard during our stay as I found him quite terrifying. If I wanted to communicate with him I did so through Auntie Lee whose calm voice would settle over the noisy house like a soft blanket. Auntie Lee came from East London and it was funny to hear her accent mixed with American euphemisms. Uncle Bernard hadn't been happy about my having a 'Winkie doll' pinned to my cardigan and asked me to remove it. I suppose it did look a bit silly, but I wasn't old enough to appreciate this. However, before we left Windsor he bought me a pendant with a picture of the Castle on which made up for the doll's removal.

At Kingston I had got to know my cousins a little better, particularly Jill who was only a year or two older than myself. She filled my head

Uncle Bernard planning his future

with her American accent ('Yeah! Gee! and Quit it!') along with stories of her school life and ballet dancing which endeared her to me. We also had in common a passion for dressing up and Jill told me of her Mexican style dress with an elasticated top that could be slipped down over the shoulders to look like a saloon girl's. I thought this was very daring and it added to the affection I felt for her.

I'd seen photographs of Uncle Bernard in Nan's dining room drawer, one of which had been taken when he was just a few months old lying on a blanket down by the dustbin. Nan said she had put him there to 'catch the sun.' Uncle Bernard was generous to me at Kingston, paying for all my trips out and treating me to a new doll the day before we left. Jill and I walked up to a shop called 'Berry Dolls' and chose one each. Mine was all decked out in green and I named her 'Becky'. I kept her for a long time as a memento of the visit.

I'd enjoyed myself with my cousins but was so looking forward to going home that I didn't think beyond saying a polite goodbye and thank you to Uncle Bernard at Waterloo, whereas Nan of course still saw him as the baby down by the dustbin. Their farewell embrace had been awkward as Uncle Bernard didn't go in for great displays of affection.

'I'll never see him again,' Nan's voice was choked with sobs as we rattled out of Waterloo. Realizing the gravity of the situation, I put Becky down and slid my arms around Nan's middle.

'Yes you will, Nan,' I assured her but, sadly, I was wrong.

When the creaking overhead announced Nan's imminent descent, I dived out of the cupboard and stood by the back door.

'I've just come in,' I replied when she asked how long I'd been there. Her eyes were a teary but I pretended not to notice this or her hanky poking out of her sleeve.

'This hayfever's a nuisance,' she said bustling about with the saucepan and cups for our coffee. 'Go on outside till I call you.'

I got myself set up on the garden path with my drawing and colouring. My 'desk' was the base of a large kitchen chair which had long since lost its top. I remember the heat of the sun on my neck and arms. Every so often the breeze got up, flapping the pages of my drawing book and the sheets on next door's line. They hung right over the fence as though cribbing my work before the creaking prop would take them back again to discuss it amongst themselves.

'Helloo, Linda.'

Mrs Whelan, my godmother, was standing by the gate. I dutifully put down my crayons and approached her. Mrs Whelan was always very well turned out in a fitted coat and a fashionable hat, a sort of boxy affair with a dark green bow tilted slightly to one side of her head. In her whispery lilt, she quizzed me as to my welfare.

'You're a good girl, are you, Linda?' she said. For some reason I was always 'Linda' to Mrs Whelan despite her having played a major role at my christening.

I always nodded of course.

'And how's your grandmother?' Mrs Whelan glanced towards the house in the hope that Nan might make an appearance, but Nan could never understand what Mrs Whelan was saying for one thing and wouldn't have been in the mood for chit-chat that day of all days for another.

When Mrs Whelan asked the inevitable question as to whether or not I would be going to Mass the following day, I said 'yes' as usual, even though I wouldn't be. Nan didn't know much about Mass, being Church of England. She had sent her youngest child, my Uncle John, to the non-Catholic school next door to our own. This was in the days before Mr Barnes' reign and John had got into all kinds of scrapes like climbing on the school roof until a policeman had been brought to 'fetch him down'.

Nan didn't understand Lent or the giving up of things for it like chocolate biscuits. Once when I tried to turn down the two she'd laid out on one of her yellow plates after school, she assured me that the Lord wouldn't want me to go hungry. I knew she had missed the point but, feeling rather peckish, had decided not to argue.

Mrs Whelan's principles about churchgoing, like those of our headmistress, were rather hard to abide by when the matter was, a lot of the time, beyond my control. Mum and Dad had a lot on their minds with Mo's situation. Dad did his best to make sure we got to Mass whenever possible, even though Will and I spent a lot of the time giggling throughout the service and generally driving him insane.

When she enquired after Mo, I told Mrs Whelan about my parents having gone to see her at Chailey and how I did not like travelling in the car much. Mrs Whelan nodded throughout and said 'Well, God Bless and don't forget your prayers.' Then off she went up the street on her thin legs.

Nan and I always went up to town on the Saturdays I stayed with her. She would change her clothes and put on a little jewellery, then give each of us a dab of scent from the bottle that had stood on the dressing table for years. All trace would have disappeared by the time we reached town except for the memory of a little cold kiss on my neck from the stopper. Scent and powder were all Nan wore in the way of make-up when she ventured out, along with the usual quick rake through of her grey hair with its natural wave. She did wear lipstick when she was younger and once more since my grandfather died. It had been on a work day at the laundry when she had wanted to 'brighten herself up a bit'. However, this was misinterpreted by one of her workmates who enquired as to who she might be 'after'. It was the sort of remark another person would have laughed off but in the case of my grandmother, who was very self-conscious, it cut very deeply. I had been earwigging on the stairs when I'd heard her relating the hateful episode in a shaky voice to Mum.

'Don't take any notice,' advised Mum. 'Miserable cows.'

But Nan did take notice of everything anyone ever said to her and never wore lipstick again.

I remember Nan putting on her 'buttercup' dress for our trip that particular Saturday; its full white skirt patterned in deep yellow flowers puffed over the bus seat as she sat down. Mine probably had flowerpots on as, even though we'd had these from the Co-op up town when we were small and outgrown them, a further batch had become available in larger sizes for myself and Mo. Therefore, they featured quite prominently throughout our childhood whatever the year.

The bus bumped its way beneath the railway bridge and along Newtown Road. The uneven terrain shot us upwards every now and then so that Nan would laugh and grasp the seat in front. It was good to see her laughing, especially after what I'd witnessed earlier.

We went past a big old house that stood in an overgrown garden beside the river. Beyond it the Stour moved slowly behind a tangle of nettles, weeds and flag iris. A little further along was the Drill Hall where the railway Christmas party was held each year for those who like myself, were still under twelve. After that you qualified for the pantomime in London. Standing on the corner of Newtown Road like a big white cake was the cinema, none the worse for its kicking from Will.

We got off at Bank Street and made our way to Sainsbury's. The store's interior was always cool even if it was boiling outside. Not surprisingly, this was one of Nan's favourite shops as it was similar to Nan herself – immaculately clean and very well presented. Fans turned in the ceiling and mosaic patterns swirled about the floor like in Willesborough Co-op. Sainsbury men wore white hats and overalls; the women's hair was netted away from their faces. Cheese was wired off onto white marble slabs; bacon and ham were sliced through with a wheel. You paid for your items at a window further down the shop, the walls of which shone in polished red brick. Nowadays, the flower design protruding for about a foot or so into the High Street is all that remains of the little Sainsbury shop that once existed in all its glory.

Crumps was another wonderful emporium with potato croquettes stacked high and all kinds of fresh dairy produce available.

Going to the pie shop was an experience I never grew tired of. The whole cooking process was done before your eyes. Sausage rolls began as long worms of pastry which were cut into sections and set into a huge oven by a long handled spade. Small meat pies and Cornish pasties were topped off, dabbed with beaten egg and sent the same way. A blast of delicious baking filled the shop each time the oven door was opened and a steaming batch fetched out onto a cooling tray. These would then be wrapped in little white bags and handed across the counter to eagerly awaiting customers. I would be drooling by that time and it was torture to have to wait until we were seated at Nan's little formica table back in Newtown before we could tuck in.

The pie shop was set in what was then a rather seedy area of town and I once saw a fight break out between a couple of red-faced men fresh from the pub. Only something as exciting as this could have dragged me away from the pie preparation. Punches and curses flew back and forth, 'Winklepicker' shoes skidded on the ground and shirts became spattered with blood. When Nan had seen the affray she'd quickly dragged me off, much to my disappointment. From then on I was always looking for a repeat performance. However, on that sunny Saturday morning of Nan's tears and my hiding in the understairs cupboard, the only incident of note in town was running into Nan's friend, Chrissie outside Woolworths. Chrissie had two chins and worked at the laundry.

'Shirkin', Chrissie?' Nan called out. Chrissie laughed when she saw Nan and made a 'go on with you' gesture like Mrs Barr sometimes did to Mum over the fence. While she and Nan commiserated over their lot at the laundry and talked of their colleagues, 'Twink' and 'Trimmy' and 'Overs' and about having to turn sheets until their arms nearly broke, I studied Chrissie. Her sandals were cream-coloured and her toes didn't quite reach the hole to poke through, but the next size up would probably have been just that much too big, I decided. A dark blue coat hid the bulk of Chrissie's figure and an amethyst brooch was pinned somewhere in the region of her left breast. I thought it funny to see Nan and Chrissie laughing and pushing each other like little girls.

In Timothy Whites, Nan purchased a waste paper bin patterned with dancers from Swan Lake. Being then quite 'ballet mad' and taking occasional lessons from Enid's Monica whenever she was home on leave from the Bluebell troupe, I had decided that the Royal Ballet was where I'd be heading later on. Naturally, I'd chosen this bin from the selection on offer and, during the bus journey home, sat turning it round, wondering how I could get from my current life to that status. I resolved to better myself and listen hard to any advice Nan had to give about manners. She was always trying to educate me about how to hold my knife and fork correctly and to keep my mouth closed when I ate instead of being 'like a cement mixer'. The mouth bit was easy enough, but the knife and fork handling was a difficult 'elbows up' manoeuvre with the formica table invariably pushing into my chest, so close would Nan set my chair for the avoidance of spillage.

'Go and get the jelly then,' she said, dabbing her mouth after we'd finished eating our lunch. I dabbed my mouth too and felt the blood rushing back into my chest as Nan released me.

The larder was cold and smelled of earth from the garden. All sorts of things were stored there, none of which, apart from the jelly in its earthenware pot, had anything to do with food. There were Wellingtons, shears, flower pots, watering cans, Brillo, Brasso, Silvo, floor polish, furniture polish, dusters, brooms, dustpans and brushes, toilet rolls (Bronco and Izal which Nan masochistically favoured over soft tissue), a small fork and trowel, a large spade and a hoe. In here, sounds from outside would drift in through the little grille in the wall - voices of neighbours or the creak of a passing bicycle.

'You gone to Timbuktu for that jelly?' called Nan.

Nan liked her jelly hard and tangerine flavoured. It didn't move when I shook the bowl or even when I turned it upside down. Eventually it squelched out onto our plates after Nan dislodged it with a spoon.

'Eat it up,' she said giving me the largest lump. 'Then I can wash the bowl and put it away.'

Later, I was sent to the shop across the green to top-up Nan's supply of Camay or talcum powder. Out of the gate I went, up the winding little street, past the garden on the corner awash with dahlias of all shapes and sizes. Their sheer number was amazing and their vivid colours surreal against the white wall of the house.

The Dutch gabled houses on Newtown Green painted by the author from an early photograph.

Newtown Green was always a gathering place for the community since the days when children had danced around the maypole. Here our school sports days were held and three-legged races run to the cheers of watching mums. The funfair would sometimes pitch up and throw its garish lights on to the Dutch gabled houses nearby. The merry-go-round left flattened yellow circles in the grass as the coloured horses, neatly stacked, moved off to another town.

A pair of wheels built by Harry Wainwright, Chief Superintendent of the railway works, in the early 1900's now stands on the green in memory of the industry that was once the hub of life here. On a rare visit from Uncle Bernard, I persuaded him and Uncle John to pose for a photograph together, or as together as they could be for they were never close. Even then they let the wheels stand between them. Now they are gone, but the green where they played as boys before life drew them apart still remains.

Next to the dark little shop I was heading for stood the bath house.

Although it has now been turned into flats, the building's attractive façade has been preserved.

No houses on Newtown had bathrooms back in the early days, so people would head across the green with their towels for a scrub up. The bath house was available three days a week for females to bathe in the mornings and males in the afternoons. The rest of the time, people made do or used the tin baths which hung in their back yards. These made wonderful boats for sailing down the river in as Will and I found once on discovering one abandoned in a field. Unfortunately, we soon realised why it had been dumped there and went home soaking wet.

After tea, I got the sideboard drawer out onto the carpet as usual. Among such items as a nutcracker, a resting mat for a tea–pot, and various collections of tea cards once belonging to my uncles, were photographs of the family mentioned before. Uncle Bernard's life was told there from his sojourn by the dustbin to his dining room in America at Christmas time with the family gathered round. There were no photographs of his wedding to Auntie Lee as they had 'just gone off and done it' in London without telling anyone. Bernard had been an attractive young man, as had my Uncle John who was pictured in his Merchant Navy uniform after getting married to Auntie Marjorie. Another photograph showed him biking across a field in Farnborough

Uncle John at Farnborough (circa 1950)

Mum aged 21

while on a visit to Bernard in the early days. In this he wears a dapper suit and a carefree smile like one who has all his life ahead of him.

There were photos of Mum from the time she was perched on a stool at two years old to various snaps of her in the WAAF. In one, she and a group of friends were gathered beneath a palm tree all wearing those unflattering halter-necked 'bobbly' swimsuits. On the back was written 'To Darling Mum and Dad.' In another she was one of four outside the billet. It read 'Kasfareet 1950. Lots of Love, Joanie.'

I had learned that Grandfather Spice hadn't wanted Mum to 'join up' and had been concerned about her a great deal of the time. He'd worried when she'd sat at the table every Saturday evening colouring her lips 'Pillar Box' red before heading off to the Corn Exchange 'hop', never mind flying to Egypt with WAAF.

Around ten o'clock with the drawer back in its place and a cup of Horlicks consumed, I followed Nan upstairs to bed. Her room was

Mum (second from left) and WAAF pals in Kasfareet, Egypt 1950

uncluttered like the rest of the house, not that she couldn't afford the occasional luxury but because she preferred an uncluttered life. She often said that if she was 'taken' tomorrow she could go peacefully, knowing she had left nothing behind. With no mess and very little paperwork - the occasional letter from Auntie Lee and a bill or two - she lived her life the way she sat on the arm of the sofa in our house – sort of half on and half off of it, not making herself too comfy in case of a sudden, hasty exit.

On the bedroom floor was a royal blue carpet and. in the corner, a wicker chair. In the wardrobe were two or three well made skirts, a sweater and a couple of blouses. There were three dresses, one being the 'buttercup,' another was a belted cream-coloured affair and the third, a patterned one with a full skirt worn at my parents' wedding. On the floor were two pairs of good walking shoes, one pair in cream the other brown with a tassle on the front. The wardrobe was also home to an upright vacuum cleaner – deafening when operated, which of course it was on a daily basis.

A vanity set in pink glass sat on the dressing table along with the aforementioned bottle of scent with a filigree top. Over the mirror hung a string of yellow beads and in the larger of the glass pots lay a necklace of ivy leaves with earrings to match. 'The Nightingale's Song', a picture of a lady in a long dress sitting at a window hung on the wall above the mantelpiece, either side of which stood two large vases, each one decorated with a peacock. It was on these that I focused before going to sleep, wondering where such beautiful birds could be found.

I had to get out on the dreaded 'po' in the middle of the night. The lack of an upstairs or even an indoor toilet was a major drawback of sleeping over at Nan's. I 'perched' with my eyes closed, trying not to let my imagination run riot. What if Grandfather decided to revisit the living room with his 'death rattle' and then wander upstairs here to walk through the door like Marley's Ghost? Then there was Great-Grannie Spice of 'the oven'. What if she chose to haunt the landing, her hair frazzled and her face burnt to a crisp? I'd be left to deal with both of these manifestations on my own as, with her hearing aid out, Nan would merely sleep on obliviously.

Back in bed, I lay awake listening to the factory clock as it chimed the hour. It was a comforting little 'tinging' sound that had been there a long time, marking the hours of other people's lives. Grandfather would have heard it chiming through the night as he lay sleepless downstairs wondering what death was like and why his life was to end so soon. Time was always moving back and forth in that house as Nan lived both in the past and the present. I often felt caught up in this myself during my visits there.

In the morning, Nan swept into the bedroom on a waft of Camay and with the usual warning over spillage, placed a cup of orange-coloured tea onto the bedside table.

'I wish I'd bought that mac after all,' she said as rain spattered the window. I hadn't been paying attention when she'd tried on a raincoat in Marks the previous day, being too concerned with doing ballet positions in the long mirror provided. Even now I was busy gazing at the 'mystery' house opposite. There was no sign of life from its upper windows, only birds flapping back and forth from the roof to the 'Monkey Puzzle' tree. I imagined myself as a bird too, flying down the chimney and up the stairs. In the bedrooms I would find wardrobes full of beautiful dresses with little hats made of sequins and feathers left over from the Charleston days.

'Are you going to drink that tea or waste it?' asked Nan bringing me back to earth with a bump.

On rainy days like that Sunday when there wasn't much to do, I'd spend my time drawing or listening to the sea in the shells on the mantelpiece. Sometimes it sounded blue, like the ocean in tropical fish book that was kept in the chimney cupboard. Also housed there was a pictorial on film stars and an ancient book called 'Stan Lynn - A Boy's Adventures In China'. There were annuals which had once belonged to my uncles, full of derring-do. One story was about a boy being chased by a lion through the jungle, *('The beast was so close to him that he could feel its hot breath on the back of his neck.')* I would read it over and over again.

Another gripping tale was that of the boy who took his father's best horse out for a ride despite being forbidden to do so. Needless to say, 'Captain' bolted and fell down a ravine breaking his neck. The boy had to confess to his father who was pictured seated behind a large desk in his study. You could almost see his moustache twitching as he received the news.

In the next picture, the father had left his desk and stood frowning out of the window as the trembling boy awaiting his punishment. All was forgiven though when the father realised it had almost been his son that was lost rather than his horse. I loved both of these stories and although the chances of being chased by a lion were minimal, I could identify with having to face the wrath of one's father.

Sometimes Nan and I would work on a 'Readicut' rug together. We'd sit for hours at a stretch, pulling the wool through the holes with the funny shaped hooks designed for the purpose.

Whenever I got the chance, I would wander into the front room to turn ornaments over in my hands. There was no clock, which added to the feeling of time suspended. I knew from earwigging that the window had been removed in order for my grandfather's coffin to be taken out.

Empty, it had been brought into the room with a series of twists and turns through the hall, but obviously this would not have been appropriate for its outward journey.

In a far corner on a hexagonal shaped table sat a pink china cup and saucer bearing the words, 'Forget Me Not'. It was unlikely that Nan would forget my grandfather or the fact that he was taken in his prime out of the window that summer morning. She had mourned him ever since and 'had only carried on for us lot'.

On the table's middle shelf sat a frilled china ashtray with a pipe stuck to it. Beneath the pipe was a picture of Margate seafront done in yellow and brown so that it looked like a small butterfly had landed on its white surface. To the left of the fireplace, two stuffed squirrels pranced either side of a sprig of nuts faded paper thin. Dad's hammer would one day fall across this down the yard and fleas run amok from the two squirrels who'd been giving them house room for some time.

The rain sounded like fingers tapping at the window and the atmosphere in the room was quite changed from the previous day when Nan had thrown open the curtains to the sun. I adjusted the little weather house on the mantelpiece so that the man beneath the door marked 'Rain' replaced the lady under 'Fine'.

'What a shame to live in the same house and never see each other,' I commented once to Nan.

'I expect plenty of people live like that,' she replied.

Nan's own marriage seemed to have worked out all right. Grandfather was a passive individual by all accounts, whereas Nan was highly strung. In that respect, they resembled what I knew of Frank and Louisa before them.

Nan's sister May married in 1933 with photos taken before and after. In a dress of dainty lace and beautiful shoes, she had been escorted up the aisle by Frank. It seems that May had fared better than Nan during childhood as she was fragile, whereas Nan or 'Ellen,' the eldest, was considered strong and responsible. In a very telling photograph, Louisa cuddles May while Ellen stands behind them with a tentative hand on her mother's shoulder.

At tea time, Nan opened the little multi-purpose unit in her kitchen. Although totally impractical by today's standards, these were quite usual back then. The top section held all her crockery, the middle with its pull

Nan's sister May with her father Frank at Willesborough Church on her wedding day in 1933

down tray was where she kept bread, butter and biscuits while the very bottom drawer housed her saucepans. Nan would load up her little wooden trolley for me to push all of three yards into the dining room.

We sat either side of the fireplace tucking into Hovis, Cornish wafers, boiled eggs which I had personally timed with the little sand-filled bottle, and the usual Fondant Fancies. Nan talked of the time I'd lived with her as a baby when Mum had joined Dad at the job in London. She had almost gone to pieces after my grandfather's death so having the care of me was a kind of therapy for her.

'I'd get you all dressed up in your pink bonnet and coat and off we'd go on the train,' she said. 'You were as good as gold; never a murmur all the way to London.'

Nan reckoned I'd been sent in my grandfather's place to be her companion.

Ellen with her mother and May in 1917

'You're my ears,' she said as always when referring to the times I'd act as interpreter for station guards or bus drivers on visits to Uncle John and Auntie Marjorie. There was a bus stop right outside Uncle John's house but Nan was never convinced that we would make the ten yard trip before the bus appeared round the corner. Therefore, we would position ourselves by the stop a good fifteen minutes ahead of time. My cousins Jane and Garry would wave politely from the window until they got fed up and replaced the curtain.

Nan spoke, as she often did, about her experiences during the war and how bombs were dropped nearby in an attempt to annihilate the railway works. Houses were destroyed and lives wrecked overnight. Two homes once stood on a patch of waste ground a little way down the road before a direct hit had wiped them out. Nan had dreaded the night raids and it was during one of these that she had squashed herself under the sink. She'd gone full term with the pregnancy and the traumatic birth, naming her stillborn daughter Mary. It would have been good for my mother to have had a sister, but sadly this wasn't to be.

Being dragged out of bed in the middle of the night and bunged down an air raid shelter seemed inconceivable to me. The worst I'd ever had to do was join the house hunt for Anne's dummy so that she and everyone else could get some sleep.

Of all Nan's remembrances, I loved to hear about her youth, before she was married.

'Tell me about the time the man chased you,' I asked. So once again Nan related the story of how she had been returning to the big house in Lenham where she'd worked as a maid when a man had sprung out of the laurel bushes. It had been her day off and having left the bus she'd set off up the long driveway. She'd hated this dark walk in winter and when there had been a rustling noise nearby hadn't dared to turn around but had run for the house frightened out of her wits. I pictured Ellen in her drop-waisted coat, her bobbed hair stuck to her face with sweat like the boy in the jungle with the beast's hot breath on the back of his neck

Ellen had hammered on the kitchen door for all she was worth. Men were sent for, men with sticks and guns. It was a house where firearms were kept for sport. Ellen herself had helped to prepare picnic baskets for the shooting parties. No-one was ever discovered in the grounds and I imagined the lady of the house making a joke of it over

Ellen in her early twenties

cards, especially when she heard it was Ellen, who had only recently fallen down the hall stairs with a tray of crockery.

'Never mind about her,' she'd said while Ellen was being checked for broken bones. 'What about my china?'

'That's what they were like,' said Nan of her employer's remark. 'They didn't care about you. Only what you could do for them. And if you didn't do it about right, out you went. I think it's because I was such a good worker that I was kept on.'

Looking back now, and knowing my grandmother to have been of a nervous disposition, I wonder about the incident of the laurel bushes. I can imagine her dreading the walk all afternoon and having got herself into a fine old state about it so that she would have been greatly surprised if there weren't at least half a dozen fiends waiting to pounce. Such was her nature.

I had decided from Nan's experiences that I had to be rich and own a large house when I grew up. If there was any telling off to be done, I would do it rather than be reprimanded myself. This would all surely fall into place when I became a famous ballerina.

I thought the title of 'Lady' or 'Dame' like 'Dame Alicia Markova' in the ballet books I borrowed from the library would suit me very well. Surely with Monica's coaching my success would only be a matter of time?

'You've come down the wrong chimney for that, I'm afraid, darling,' said Nan when I voiced my hopes and dreams. As she cleared away the tea things, I was left gazing in to the hearth realising for the first time just where I was on the social scale and how far away those dreams might actually be.

I stayed overnight at Nan's less frequently as I grew older. The hours would drag for me in the evening, especially in the winter when we couldn't sit outside. The rooms where no fire was lit, namely all of those other than the dining room, would be freezing. There was no heating in our own house either, but at least you could get warmed up in a hot bath even if it meant having your brother at the other end and baby sister plonked in the middle while your mum 'got on'.

By the time those Sunday evenings rolled around at Nan's I would be waiting anxiously for Dad to collect me. His smile would chase away

Myself with cousins Jane and Gary at Gravesend

the feelings of melancholy which seeped through the house when it rained, for then the noise of the sea in the shells on the mantelpiece would sound wistful and the ocean grey and lonely. After a hurried kiss and hug from Nan, we would go off down the path together, Dad and I, past the forlorn little yard. Part of me would rejoice at being once again in his vibrant company and in the immediacy of my young life; another part remained with Nan and 'Ellen,' the invisible thread that joined us, tugging at my heart.

A Flame Extinguished

Autumn. Ankle deep in leaves, we crunched our way round the boards to school; our cheeks flushing red and our mouths steaming like chimneys. The bonfire on the green out front was growing bigger by the day with neighbours' rubbish. Rupert and Alan from over the road had been arranging old mattresses, clothes, newspapers and broken furniture around a central wooden pole dug into the ground. Branches of Patty's cherry tree were propped against a rotting sofa, her dad having abandoned his radios in favour of a hacksaw when Mrs Cherry complained about the tree stealing her light. His grey cap had been visible nodding back and forth behind the wall as he'd worked. Close up, the newly-cut branches smelled sweet against the odour of decay from within the mountain of junk.

Sighting Rupert over at the fire after school one afternoon, I couldn't eat my tea quick enough to get out there with a box of old newspapers.

'What's the rush?' asked Mum. 'You'll get indigestion.'

The Pattersons were picking over some old clothes left in a cardboard box before Rupert could stuff them in behind the branches. Anything the Pattersons fancied went over the road to their house it seemed. Mum said she couldn't help feeling sorry for them and they could have had all our old bits if she'd known. However, passing any kind of charity onto Mrs Patterson might prove difficult when only a few weeks before, Mum had thrown a jug of water at a clutch of her 'nuisances' loitering around our back gate.

'Don' aff to!' Valerie had shouted when Mum had told them to scarper.

'It's a free country!' another had exclaimed.

'Not round here it's not!' Mum had said, heading out with the jug.

She didn't catch any of them but Valerie had been wearing her mac as usual so it wouldn't have mattered if she had.

When I got to the green, little Kitty Patterson was pulling out newspapers from the fire and throwing them over the place. 'Marilyn Monroe found dead' was the headline she clutched in her fist, while the Cuban Missile Crisis flapped carelessly across the green. Kitty's nose was running and her coat was done up wrongly.

Rupert pulled out a handful of stuffing from a busted sofa and turned to me.

'Oi, do you know what this looks like?' he asked.

I went to move quickly to his side, but then decided to stroll over casually. My new strategy of ignoring him since the letter business must have been having some effect, I decided, for him to summon me thus.

'No. What?' I asked, studying his face rather than the yellow fluff he held in his hands. I noticed that a few freckles dotted his cheeks and his eyes were a light brown beneath dark lashes. Our sleeves were touching and I wished we could remain there together, locked in time. I assumed he was about to share some gem of scientific wisdom gained from secondary school so I tried to look serious and intelligent.

'An old man's arse hair,' he said with a great guffaw.

With my face as red as Kitty's legs, I got to my feet and slunk away.

Bally Useless

After lessons with Monica became more regular, I grew brave enough to treat the school to the occasional dance routine at the Friday concert. This was just a series of steps really with nothing linking them, but of course that didn't deter me from flying back and forth in my jumper and navy knickers. I once caused a titter and a considerable amount of flinching when I decided to squeeze in another 'grand jete' before reaching the front row.

'I've got something for you,' said Mrs Lucas, having watched one of my performances. 'Come and see me after dinner tomorrow.'

Mrs Lucas was one of the dinner ladies who'd taken a liking to me for some reason and occasionally passed on dresses from her niece. I'd had an 'owl' patterned one and a pink candy stripe. I duly presented myself at the kitchen door, thinking this was the sort of thing she had in mind.

'Tell your mum I hope she's not offended,' said Mrs Lucas, handing me something in a paper bag. Imagine my delight when I saw that it was a leotard!

I couldn't see why Mum would have been offended. After all, the red leotard wasn't for her any more than the owl dress had been or the pink stripey one, the skirt of which had been ripped from the bodice when it got caught in the wheel of Will's go-kart. I had a real leotard at last! I was delighted that Mrs Lucas had taken an interest in my chosen career and couldn't wait to get home to try it on. However, disappointment hit in a big way when the thing would hardly stretch up as far as my shoulders. Determined to get into it at all costs, I managed to yank it on. The only drawback being that I couldn't straighten up without almost cutting myself in half 'down below'. Undaunted, I launched my round-shouldered self across the landing but the unforgiving suit prevented me from raising my head enough to see where I was going. I pitched into the bathroom wall and slid to the floor like a kamikaze hand-glider.

Simple exercises at the barre, or the 'banister' to be precise, were impossible without correct upright posture. I therefore tried to concentrate on leg positions only, but again the suit had me in its forward grip and this proved far too uncomfortable. Once more, I sank to the floor in pain, curled up like a caterpillar or one of the elasticated slipperettes Nan wore in summer, temporarily discarded while she attended to her corn.

With great sadness I removed the vicious garment and threw it into a corner. I had hoped to wear the leotard on my next lesson with Monica but now it was back to knickers after all. I considered what my heroine, Anna Pavlova, would have done in the same circumstances. I had read about her baptism of fire when she was taken to 'The Sleeping Beauty' at eight years old. She hadn't allowed anything to put her off her chosen career and neither would I. Therefore I continued practising despite the setback and got my leg as high as it would go against the banister.

'You'll split yer difference in a minute,' observed Mum passing by with an armful of laundry.

'At least I'm getting lessons from a Bluebell girl,' I thought to myself, 'Not everyone can say that.'

Neither could I for very much longer. When I next went to Enid's, Monica was sitting at the kitchen table in her Co-op overall. Usually, she would be dressed in her leotard with a skirt over it perhaps and her shoes on ready.

'Bad news, love,' she said. 'Mum's having some friends round. We can't practice today.'

I was flattered by the 'we', imagining myself on a par with the members of Monica's dance troupe. All the same, I couldn't hide my disappointment, but there was worse to come. In his basket by the fireplace, Matey put his head down on his paws as though in anticipation of what was to follow.

'What about the shed?' I suggested.

'Not a good idea, love,' said Monica.

'But I've got my shoes and everything.'

'I know and I'm glad you're here,' said Monica. 'I've been wanting to have a chat.'

Ah, perhaps all is not lost then, I thought to myself. Maybe she was going to suggest I was ready for an exam. Well, it was high time. I'd been going to her for weeks, twice a week sometimes and when we did our show in the summer Mrs Cherry had said I was a 'born dancer.' Already I could see my trophy standing beside one of Dad's on the sideboard. Monica had several in her living room along with a photo that had been taken holding one of them. Enid had been dusting it the last time I came round, a cigarette in the corner of her mouth.

'You're very graceful,' went on Monica, 'You try really hard, but the trouble is you're getting far too tall for ballet.'

'I'm not that tall,' I argued with a tremor in my voice. 'I'm really not.'

'You haven't stopped growing yet,' she said. 'Nowhere near. Honestly, love. It would be a waste of time to carry on. Besides, I'm going away with the Bluebells again soon.'

'But…what about the Co-op?' I asked, my throat closing. 'You've got an overall and everything.'

Monica threw back her head and screeched as though she's spotted something hilarious on the ceiling. 'Oh, you are funny!'

I failed to see what there was to laugh about. I didn't expect the Co-op handed out overalls willy-nilly.

'Mum just got me in there for the summer,' soothed Monica, her head on one side as though looking at me from a slightly different angle would assuage my disappointment. 'I'm re-joining the company in London on Monday.'

The 'company' meant of course the girls, the costumes, the lights, the stage, the music, the life. Matey let out a sigh as I crumbled inside.

'You could always learn Modern,' said Monica encouragingly. 'There's a place up town.'

Yes, there was a place up town, but it was two and six a lesson after bus fare. Then there were shoes and leotards, proper ones that fitted, school knickers just wouldn't do there.

'Can you teach me when you come back again?' I asked hopefully, but Monica shook her head.

'I don't know when that'll be. We're going on to Paris after London, you see.'

I saw alright. I saw the light go out on my dancing future and could hardly bare to put one foot in front of the other to walk to the gate.

Mum was up to her elbows in flour when I arrived home with tears running down my face.

'What are you bawling about now?' she asked. I told her about Monica's treachery.

'I could have told you that in the first place. You've come down the wrong chimney for that, duck.'

That bloody chimney.

Fireworks

'Ye'll get sense yet, you lot.'

Dad was giving his opinion of the November 5th celebrations as he passed us all waving our sparklers in the back yard.

'Oh, Sull!' said Mum turning one with Anne.

'Heh! I breaks me back for money to keep ye all and ye sends it up in smoke! My Jaysis, I dunno why I bothers me head.'

'Oh, Dad, don't go in!' we begged. 'We want you to do the fireworks!'

'Fireworks me ass.'

It was better to wait until Dad was ready to light the blue touch paper rather than ignite his own by mithering further before he'd eaten.

'Mudder o' God!' he said half an hour later as the first of our spindly rockets whooshed up past the shed. 'That's an hour's wages gone, Lizzie.'

'Look! It's still burning!' yelled Will.

'Burning me bastard pocket, that's all,' said Dad.

'Oooh, that's pretty, isn't it?' said Mum as hundreds of little stars sprayed from a 'Diamond Pyramid'.

'Stand back out of it,' warned Dad, so we all backed off a few feet as he returned to light the next firework in line – a Roman Candle. The Pyramid, not being quite finished, did a final explosion shocking Dad almost out of his boots.

'My Jaysis!' he said running back to where we stood screaming with laughter.

'Mind my trellis, Sull!' said Mum as Dad began hammering a Catherine Wheel in beside the honeysuckle. 'It only needs a pin, duck. Not a great big nail like that!'

'How can I see a pin in the bastard dark, woman!' replied Dad.

'I don't expect it'll turn now,' said Mum.

She was right – it didn't, only shrieked like a banshee as sparks flew from its tail. It was found still nailed the following morning with a big burn mark on the trellis and much of the honeysuckle scorched into the bargain.

'That's yer lot,' said Dad. 'Get out me sight, the lot o'ye.'

Will and I joined the gathering out front for the grand lighting of the bonfire by Patty's dad. Patty, who needed the toilet but didn't want to miss the event, was holding herself and hopping about on one leg.

People were still bringing stuff out to throw on. The Patterson's guy was rather macabre, being just an old pillow tied at one end with string so that it resembled a sandbag from a scaffold. It didn't take long to disintegrate, folding over sadly and collapsing through the flames.

We weren't allowed to 'guy', as this came under 'begging' in Dad's book. If he had sighted us outside the chip shop with our crayoned sign and stuffed jumper with a pair of old socks pinned on, there would have been hell, rather than a penny to pay. Lucky then that Mum had seen us emerging from the shed with our woolly passenger slumped on Will's go-kart and nipped our idea in the bud.

In the light of the flames, the faces of neighbours took on different aspects. No-one spoke much, they just watched as the cherry tree branches hissed and snapped and sparks flew up into the night air. There was a kind of fitness to old things dying on the fire as there was to dancing at the club on New Year's Eve, when hands and waists were clutched to music as the old year was replaced by the new.

Hell on Wheels

My hopes of becoming a ballerina and marrying Rupert lay in cinders like the bonfire on the green after Guy Fawkes Night. However, like a phoenix from the ashes, it wasn't long before new hope rose in the shape of a pair of roller skates produced by Dad from God knows where. Skating was clearly the way to go! I could practice on roller skates and graduate to the ice when I was older; it was all skating in one form or another, I decided. Rupert would wish he'd paid me more attention when he saw me on TV dancing off across the ice with my trophy!

Admittedly, there were one or two minor problems with these skates. Firstly, they might possibly have been in a fire. They were a little rusty and didn't have any laces or anywhere to put the laces as a matter of fact as the front leather sections were missing. Secondly, much like the BR parcel lorry that we once travelled to Chailey in, there was just the base and wheels, which having no rubbers on, were rather noisy. I couldn't do much about this but I improvised with regard to the laces by threading pieces of bandage through the metal eyelets either side of the base. I tied them as tightly as I could over each foot. That done, I moved gingerly across the green to Patty's fence which seemed like a good place to launch off from, as the path then sloped down to the square.

Hurling myself forward, I rapidly gained momentum so that the recently polished car belonging to Mr Todd, a neighbour, grew nearer by the second. Its front grille and fender seemed to take on a sinister grin as I hurtled towards it out of control with my own face set in a grimace of terror.

I shot off the kerb and flew across the square, my wheels sparking on the concrete as I landed. A second or two later I hit the car with a thud, my legs going east and west as I slid to the ground. In my head I could hear that slow, mocking trumpet that plays when when things go wrong in the 'Carry On' films. 'Wah, Wah, Wah, Waaaaahhhhhh!'

After unpicking the knots in the bandages and re-positioning the skates that had slipped round behind my feet, I headed, shaken but undeterred, up the alley. Here the sound from the unprotected wheels was quite deafening and soon had Mrs Todd yelling from her bedroom window for me to 'Clear off out of it' as she was just about to put the baby down for a nap.

'Sorry,' I said, highly embarrassed. Only the previous day Mrs Todd had remarked to Mum on how grown up I was getting. I had obviously blown my street cred with her over this, not to mention the finger marks down her husband's car bonnet.

Clinging to the wall, I hurried back down the alley as quickly as I could. Again, the skates seemed to take on a life of their own and bore me along 'À toute vitesse'. Off the step I shot, speeding past Enid's doing a sort of backstroke through the air. I grasped at the hedge in desperation. Both feet left the ground momentarily as I jerked to a halt and crashed to the pavement. Matey's big head appeared through the hedge above my face. Panting excitedly, his pink tongue lolling, he no doubt thought this another fun exercise like those I'd performed in his kitchen with Monica while he looked on from outside the back door.

Meanwhile, Dad must have been observing my antics as he turned up blocking out the sun.

'Pack that game up,' he said. 'Ye hasn't a clue. Ye'll break ye bastard neck, ye nannygoat.'

I struggled with the knotted bandages and handed him the useless skates. Sniffing, I limped home as another career hope was slung back into the lorry and driven away.

A Sweet Sin

At school, the usual lead-up to Christmas had begun. One morning in Assembly, the headmistress was talking about remembering the souls in Purgatory and how we should never forget Mass on Sunday even if it was cold outside and we didn't feel like getting out of our warm beds. Jesus, she reminded us, had travelled around preaching no matter what the weather and if we were cold and uncomfortable on the walk to church, we should offer this up to God in atonement for our sins.

The hymn was 'Star of the Sea', about the Blessed Virgin guarding those in danger. I imagined the starlight across the water and the sound of its gentle whoosh, like in Nan's shells. Dad had announced he was taking us to Cork on a visit in the spring and I remembered the last time we sailed the Irish sea, a huge expanse of shiny black, lit by the moon and the foamy wake behind as our ship, the 'Innisfallen' had cut through it.

So busy was I with the sea and Ireland that I didn't hear my name being called until Winnie nudged me. It was someone's birthday and the headmistress had apparently elected me to go out to the staff room for the sweet tin. Mounting the elephant's foot, a requirement of the birthday person, was Norman, one of the younger pupils.

I never officially got to stand on the elephant's foot as my birthday fell during the summer holidays, but to make up for this I would have a quick go on it while passing through the hall on the way back from the toilet during a lesson. The last time I had done so the piano tuner had been over in the corner, I hadn't realised his presence but he'd heard me of course, his head on one side listening, his blind dark eyes rolling to the rafters. He'd reached into the piano and struck a dull note like a reprimand which sent me scuttling off.

The foot, covered in burgundy velvet, frequently had its toes polished by Mr Pick. After the poor elephant's demise, its foot had obviously fallen victim to the Victorians' passion for stuffing things, much like Nan's squirrels.

I made my way past the lines of children singing 'Happy Birthday' while Norman stood on the foot, red-faced and twisting his hands in embarrassment. Some of the smaller girls were swaying to and fro on their heels as they sang. It had become the pattern. If one started, others tended to follow.

Steaming macs dripped onto the floorboards in the lobby as I passed through to the main entrance. The teachers had once gathered in a little room off the passageway that linked the two schools until Mr Barnes had claimed it as much needed classroom. They had all been seated around the fireplace when I had gone there on an errand once and I'd thought how cosy it looked. The new staff room wasn't much more than a makeshift shed in the playground, which was still white with frost even though dozens of feet had traversed it that morning.

Fumes from a paraffin heater filled the room and Miss's familiar blue mac was spread out over the back of a chair to dry. On the table were various piles of exercise books, some open and marked with red ink. Empty cups and saucers lay on a tray along with the sugar bowl and milk. On the shelf above the table stood the sweet tin, patterned in blue with horizontal stripes. From a window in its centre a girl smiled out gleefully at being the guardian of its contents.

Having arrived in double quick time, I had a few moments for something I had always desired to do, namely to have a peep inside the tin. I unscrewed the lid gently to find such delights inside as 'Fruit Bon-Bons' which everyone knew were expensive and usually eaten by grown ups. Patty's granddad always had a packet of these to hand when we visited. Aniseed Twists and Liquorice Allsorts also lay inside on a bed of Fruit Pips. The whole delicious looking treasure was reflected against the tin's golden interior. My mouth watered at the sight and smell. A single orange and black striped Allsort would surely not be missed?

I shoved it in my mouth, wishing straight away that I had not done so as, rather than shrink, it became the biggest sweet I'd ever eaten in my life and seemed to grow by the second. This was my punishment of course. I would never be able to stop eating it and be found out and expelled. My father's wrath! I remembered the boy and Captain, the horse.

After what seemed hours of frantic chewing, the sweet was gone but I was now in sheer panic thinking of the liquorice odour on my breath and the headmistress being able to smell it from twenty yards away if she couldn't already. I pictured her waiting in the hall sniffing the air and tapping the floor with her foot in expectation of my return.

A piece of thawed snow fell from the roof to the ground outside the door making me jump out of my skin. I turned and stepped right into the paraffin heater, knocking it for six. Expecting the place to burst into flames any second, I whimpered with fright as I carefully lifted the heater back up. Mercifully, nothing had spilled onto the floor but I suspected there would be flames one day where I was going. I had really sinned here and no mistake.

With my face as hot as the heater, I returned to the hall and handed the tin over to the headmistress who was in full flow about the order of the 'Poor Clares' and how there was a special box available that week for any donations we might want to bring in. Thus, preoccupied, she did not study my face at all when she took the tin from me.

I knew I ought to go to confession but the prospect was terrifying. I was in a real quandary as, if I did not confess and died soon after, I would surely end up in Purgatory at least, if not in hell itself. All I could hope for was the sort of death that comes after a long illness so that I could at least have time to get Extreme Unction. I could then whisper the theft of the Allsort quietly to the priest concerned; hopefully not Father Joe but Father Ambrose who had little to do with our school or its teachers, being often in Ireland on Retreat.

I spent all day agonising in this way, wishing I'd never touched the bloody sweet tin and that I wasn't a Catholic, like Hilary for example who stole things all the time, like my cocoon, and got away with it. My punishment was going to be living with myself, I decided, until the day a dove hovered at my window like in the picture of Extreme Unction. Only then would I confess. Meanwhile, I would have to do as Jane Eyre intended when asked by Mr Brocklehurst as to how she would avoid going to hell – namely 'Keep healthy and not die'.

Year Ends

Our bedroom windows were patterned with frost each morning and the scraping of the porridge saucepan would be followed by Mum's yell for us to get up. Huddled in our dressing gowns, Will and I would descend, thumping each other in a bad temper at having to leave our warm beds. As we laced our shoes and pulled up our socks, we envied Anne playing with her toys by the fire.

The walk to school was numbingly cold, even with Mum's hand knits beneath our macs. The air, sharp with frost and coal dust, stung our faces as we gathered with the other kids in the playground. The headmistress would encourage us to run around and keep warm, her whistle poised for those who disobeyed. There was usually an icy slide in one of the playgrounds with kids lining up for a turn to skid across it. Squabbling would invariably break out over queue-jumping and fights would follow, causing the headmistress to give a long blast on her whistle before swooping down to yank the offenders apart. The guilty would have to stand in the hall on the chalked 'white line' all through the next playtime and, unless granted a last minute reprieve, face the dreaded 'Cane'.

The last day of school before the Christmas holidays was always exciting. Even the railway crossing man would have a decoration hung in his window. During the morning, we would design our paper doilies for the afternoon party fare, which we were allowed to eat at our desks. There would be games in the hall such as 'Pass the Parcel', or 'Parcel Parcel' as I had called it first, and 'Musical Chairs'. When I was very young I dreaded this game and, on being caught out 'chair-less', would continue to run pointlessly around those seated until told I was 'out', then slope away red-faced, eyes brimming.

There was a fancy dress parade one year. Mrs Lucas had given me a fringed, satin frock for 'dressing up' in and Mum made me a headdress with a feather on and a long cigarette holder to carry. With safety pins,

Dad assisting Rolf Harris at a future Christmas lights ceremony
(Photograph courtesy of the Kentish Express)

she altered a suspender belt to fit and produced a pair of stockings, which, needless to say, were far too big. She and Nan thought I might steal the show as a 'Charleston girl', but the competition was won by a classmate called Josephine who went as a Christmas cracker, covered from head to toe in red and green tulle nipped in at two places for the effect. I was greatly disappointed but hers really was a terrific costume. I soon whipped off my stockings, which had gathered at my ankles and consoled myself with jelly and cake.

One of the first harbingers of the Yuletide was the parade around the streets. This was sponsored by the hospitals, the fire brigade and the British Legion. The floats would be escorted by the Territorial Army band. Its distant thump would draw Will and I, all excited, out to the front where shadowy figures wearing huge false heads would rattle collection boxes. We joined our neighbours along the kerb as Father Christmas passed by along with various elves and fairies.

The parade culminated in the switching on of the Christmas lights in the High Street, usually by a celebrity of some sort. Rolf Harris was to oblige a few years later with Dad assisting in his capacity as 'bouncer' by keeping the crowd at bay.

Nana Spice once had a party dress made for me as a Christmas present. I would have preferred a ballet dress for the Friday concerts – even though the lessons had dried up, I would still continue to float about as if I knew what I was doing. However, Nan felt that a party dress would be of more use and, as she was paying, I couldn't very well argue.

We found the dress material in a little shop in New Street. It was a lovely sky blue satin with a fern leaf pattern. A layer of net in the same shade was to be stitched over the top and the sleeves were to be puffed. Jean, a relative of Nan's, was a seamstress and mother of two invisible boys, Matthew and Anthony. During our first visit, while I was being measured, Jean would periodically yell up the stairs for her sons to come down and say hello. As there was no response either then or when we returned for my fitting a couple of weeks later, I was left wondering whether these boys existed at all or if Jean had been spending too long at her sewing machine in her tiny, half-lit dining room.

Real enough though and not far from Jean's was Hansons, the wonderful fish and chip emporium where Nan treated me to lunch. 'Cod and chips twice, roll and butter, two cups of tea' was our order.

The tabletops were green like the floor and fish shapes set in the frosted glass gave the impression that we were sitting in a giant aquarium.

Nan would always keep her hat on throughout lunch. She was very proud of the brown, furry affair which matched the collar on her coat. We chatted above the clatter of plates and cutlery with Nan cupping her ear every now and then against the din.

'I'll be glad when it's all over, won't you?' she said to the waitress about Christmas. This remark took some of the shine off the approaching celebrations for me. I had thought everyone looked forward to Christmas and was surprised to hear that Nan saw it all as something that had to be endured.

'It's different when you're old,' she said, on seeing my expression.

'But you're not old Nan,' I argued. She just laughed and told me I was lovely and to 'take my elbows off the table please.'

It was true though, Nan didn't seem old to me, not when I compared her to Patty's Nan who was very old indeed and just sat in her chair all day licking her mouth like a cat. I'd last been to her house on Patty's birthday; it was down a little path at the back of Albemarle Road. The garden had been full of cabbages, sweet peas and white butterflies. Patty's granddad had given her a ten shilling note as a present and done most of the talking. The old lady was only able to shake her head a bit and gaze around the ceiling as though Patty and I were butterflies that had flown in through the window instead of two girls standing next to her.

I studied my Christmas list to renew my spirit after Nan's dampener:

Dad – Diary and pencil
Mum – Devonshire violets scent
Nan – Powder puff in little bag
Mo – Writing book and pen
Will – 2 plastic soldiers – 1 green, 1 brown
Anne – Winkie doll with earrings

These were obtained from Woolworths with a few pennies left over for wrapping paper out of the ten shilling note Dad had given me for purchases. Nan only ever did a few cards and never bothered with a tree or decorations as she always spent Christmas Day with us, not wanting 'the mess'.

The High Street windows were full of tinsel and cheer. We visited

Santa's grotto in Lewis and Hyland's even though I was probably a bit big by then to be sitting on his knee. I was delighted with my gift, a colouring book and pencils.

Nan's Christmas treat to herself was a new corset or 'stays' from Strange's, who she said supplied the best quality. These were all hooks and bones and looked grossly uncomfortable to me.

'I can't wait to get home and get these stays off,' Nan would say after a trip up town or to our house, but she ordered her annual set nevertheless.

Nan had a large bust, which her bra, or 'bray' as she called it, did its level best to control. Invariably, the 'brays' and 'stays' would be found drying on the oven door pending completion of her daily wash down. They would be dried outside in the summer on a small line in the backyard near the door, never down the garden with the bed sheets and the pillows 'for all to see'.

I could hardy contain my excitement on returning to Jean's for the dress when, at last, it was ready. There it lay on the sofa beneath a layer of tissue. I stepped into it while Jean yelled anew at her two invisible sons to come down and be sociable. When she zipped the dress up with a flourish, the satin felt rich and cold against my skin.

'Stand over there,' said Jean. I duly went to the window where I spied a boy's bike and a go-kart in the yard. So her sons weren't imaginary after all.

'Lovely,' cooed Nan. 'You look a picture.'

Jean tugged at the hem a bit and straightened the netting over the skirt.

'Sleeves not too tight?' she asked.

'No.' There was a good half-inch between the puffed satin and my bony arm.

'Won't fit for long,' said Jean. 'Make the most of it.'

'Go in the hall and look in the glass,' said Nan.

I did so and could see the bodice down to where the netting billowed out from the waist. Unlike the bridesmaid dress hired by Mrs Drake, it was mine to keep. In the mirror was a different me, someone new.

'Nice hair and clothes make a person,' Nan would often say. 'Don't ever forget that.'

From above came a scuttling noise and the quick closing of a bedroom door. Was it the biker or the go-karter? I was never to know.

'Can I wear it home?' I asked.

'As long as you're careful,' said Nan opening her clip-top purse to settle up with Jean.

I skipped along the pavement with my coat open to the winter sun and Nan marching behind me. One of my favourite meals at Nan's – tinned chicken in sauce from Marks with peas and mash – was on the menu for lunch, along with creamed rice for pudding. In a burst of excitement over this prospect, the dress and life in general, I took off at a run and embraced the nearest lamp post with joy a little too late to see the 'Wet Paint' sign.

As if that wasn't enough bad luck for one day, while we were standing in the bus queue outside Sainsbury's with Nan looking fed up and me grizzling over my paint-stained dress, some lads decided to use Nan's fur hat as a rugby ball. Full of seasonal cheer, they whipped it from her head and began passing it to each other across the High Street having a right old game.

In a highly emotional state by now, I demanded the hat back with menaces. This had no effect on the pranksters of course and it was only when they grew tired of their game that they drop kicked it back in our general direction. Nan was all of a doodah by then and I was fit to kill. Mercifully, the bus arrived and by the time we reached Nan's front gate we had both calmed down considerably. Nan's hat was none the worse for the incident after she had brushed it up a bit. As for my dress, all was not quite lost. Nan produced a pair of little gold handled scissors from her sewing kit and carefully snipped the net away from the waistband. It wasn't quite the dress it had been but was still very pretty.

'Never mind duck,' said Mum when I related my misfortune at the tea table.

'Ye nannygoat,' opined Dad from behind the Kent Messenger.

On Christmas Eve, Dad would bring in a turkey complete with feathers and floppy neck. It was a grisly sight and not for the squeamish, neither was the smell when Dad cleaned it out. In fact, the kitchen was best avoided entirely during the whole nasty process. If you needed the toilet it was best to go via the seldom used door in the far corner of the front room giving onto the hall. If Dad caught you sneaking along there, as happened to me once, he would chase you with bloodied newspaper and roar with laughter as you tried to secrete yourself beneath the hanging coats. You could say this was how he got his own back for all those mornings spent sniggering at his misfortunes.

For several days it seemed that the whole house was given over to the turkey. From its arrival, a slumped, forlorn heap on the lino, to the horror of its plucking and drawing, to the smell of its cooking which permeated through the house all night, to it being served up finally on Christmas Day with Dad eagerly brandishing a knife and a sharpening tool. It would reappear on the tea table with mustard and pickle and again on Boxing Day with mash, until there was only the carcass left. Dad would seek this out on his return from the club, assuring us that there was plenty left if you knew where to look.

'Fine bird that,' he proclaimed once as Mum had deposited the last few dry bones into the dustbin. 'Ye could make a soup from them bones, ye waster.'

On Christmas Eve before sleep, Mo and I would run through a question and answer session regarding our gifts. I usually knew what everyone would get in their pillowcase, having been present at the delivery from the catalogue and at the wrapping up by Mum in front of the fire. One year, after severe questioning, I dropped too large a hint that Mo's gift, which I knew to be a building set, was something white and made of plastic pieces.

'It's not a building set is it?' she asked with disappointment in her voice. 'I don't want that, why have I got that?'

I explained how Mum had ordered it for Will and then seen a Meccano set on sale at the Post Office so had thought that Mo would like the building set instead.

'There's loads you can make with it,' I said. 'I'll help you.'

This was met with a stony silence.

'Well? What are my clues?' I asked.

'It's small,' Mo said grumpily. 'It's got a glass face and a strap but it's not a watch. So there.'

In the early morning light, I helped Mo to sit up and began ferreting for the pillowcases, which were usually deposited either at the ends of our beds or somewhere on the floor. Mo tugged at hers with her 'good' hand while I doggedly continued to extol the virtues of a

'Betta Builda' and the hours of fun we'd have together making a whole town. But Mo was no more impressed when she opened the gift than before and had abandoned it by the afternoon in favour of a 'Fuzzy Felt'. My watch didn't fare much better as it was boiled in the single-tub a few days later when I'd left it in my pyjama pocket by accident.

I had been given a mosaic pattern game with which I was delighted. The colours were fascinating; the same as the water jug on the dinner tables at school – shiny pink, yellow, blue, silver and green. However, I didn't endear myself to Dad when he located a missing ball beneath his foot one morning a few days later.

'My Jaysis, ye has me killed!' he exclaimed, hopping along the landing, nursing his foot and accusing us all of setting booby traps. He flung the ball out of the window and I spent the rest of the day hunting for it to no avail.

On Christmas Day lunchtime, Dad took us children down to the club. We were delighted to be allowed into the bar where beer spilled to the wooden floor and smoke rose up above paper chains like a fog.

'Give us a carol, Bill,' encouraged someone.

We sipped our Vimtos and watched as Dad, accompanied by old Jack on the organ, took the mike and launched into 'O, Come All Ye Faithful' followed by 'Hark The Herald Angels sing'. Everyone joined in but it was Dad's voice that rose to the roof. He sang with passion, as though this were his own Christmas prayer in gratitude for all that he had; for us and our Mum, for his life and for the future.

'Merry Christmas. God Bless,' he said, raising a glass to everyone. His ears were flaming red as usual and there was such an honesty to him as he stood there in his baggy old cardigan that I will remember the scene for the rest of my life.

Despite her lack of enthusiasm in Hanson's, Nan seemed to enjoy herself to some degree on Christmas Day that year. While we had been down the club, she and Mum accepted Mrs Drake's invitation for a sherry next door and had only returned a few minutes before our arrival back home.

'Oh, ack! I could have sworn that chair was there, Joanie!' Nan exclaimed after landing on the floor with only one fluffy new slipper on. We were all hysterical.

Unusually, Mum had things completely back to front with the dishing up. This worked in my favour as I was served first and got a good amount of roast potatoes, even though they were slightly on the crispy side. In paper hats, Mum and Nan, who was still baffled over her miscalculation of the chair's position, moved from oven to table with dishes and tea cloths. Every so often they would be attacked by another spasm of laughter so that the back of a chair would be gripped or a cupboard leaned against for support.

Dad sharpened the carving knife and attacked the turkey. We all pulled crackers and tucked in, even Nan, who was usually so delicate when eating, burst out laughing with a hot potato in her mouth which started us all off again.

After lunch, Nan regaled us with stories of heady days spent working at the George Hotel and the Saracen's Head. One fellow had a car and would take young Ellen and friends for drives down to Hythe and Folkestone on their evenings off.

'I remember dancing to 'Limelight' with Sid Blizzard,' she said, wistfully. Sid's name alone had us all helpless, even before Nan had got to the part where he would 'bend her back over his arm'.

Despite her social occupation when she was young, Nan had never quite got the hang of smoking, yet if I said she smoked like a chimney this would also be true as she did exactly that. On the rare occasions that she took one of Mum's Weights and lit it, she would hold the smoke in without inhaling and then puff it out the side of her mouth. As children, we may have tittered over this and 'Sid Blizzard', but these endearing memories rank very highly indeed in my 'collection'.

At Christmas teatime, prior to turkey sandwiches, Dad, usually still sporting his paper hat, would allow us a drink from the 'bar'. This consisted of four bottles standing under the Christmas tree on the sideboard. We would choose from the sherry, port, whisky or egg flip and were given a tiny amount in the lid or the bottom of a glass, which we thought was great.

'Good luck,' Dad would say, raising his glass.

'Good luck,' said we, already considering ourselves the luckiest family in the street.

New Year's Eve at the club was very exciting to us children. The fun began from the moment you took a hat out of the box by the door on your way in. These hats were made of what I call 'egg box' material in various colours and were shaped like miniature bowlers, trilbies and policeman's helmets. Others were pirate or fez-shaped, topped off with a feather. They were for children really, but some adults weren't averse to popping one on like Mr Clough, for example, whose bulldog features were softened by a little orange trilby worn at a jaunty angle.

Music from the band thumped you in the chest and made you want to dance, even if you couldn't jive like the grown-ups. I loved the 'Gay Gordons' and once got partnered with Mr Drake who didn't dance at all but walked his way through. Twisting my hand in his gnarled old fingers, he'd shake his leg a bit here and there, blinking and puffing away on his fixed roll-up. During the 'Okie Kokie' he put the wrong limb in and out and was still 'turning around' while everyone else was charging into the centre.

As always, people would comment on how alike Mum and Mo were. Now and again, someone would push two shillings or half a crown between Mo's fingers so that she was quite wealthy by the end of the evening. As with the carols, Dad never needed much encouragement to sing. One year, he gave his rendition of 'Danny Boy'. The sad tale of love and death turned people's eyes misty for a moment or two between the jive and the twist. Then there was applause and whooping and a pint passed along. We were proud and happy because it was only a song and the words weren't real. Our Dad would never die and neither would any of us either.

A Little Too Much Information

The council men had cut the grass again. It was as though a sweet new tablecloth had been thrown over the green. I lay on a blanket watching a plane moving through the sky, its white tail expanding from thin to fluffy. Over by the wall, Mrs Cherry was complaining to Mum about the grass being left to blow all over the place. It was true – the street looked like the barber's floor on a Saturday morning.

I turned back to the magazine I had been reading. It was one of the latest batch passed on to Mum by Mrs Drake and contained adverts for corsets, Carnation corn pads, Scholl sandals, rubber pants and long knickers like Miss wore. The short stories were way over my head but I was fascinated by the medical problem pages and the adverts for something called 'Tampax internal sanitary protection.' What on earth was that? Protection against what? 'Internal' meant 'inside' didn't it? Inside where for heaven's sake and it must be inside a girl because there was one in the picture. Why would she want to wear it inside her, whatever it was? It was a real puzzle to me, that advert.

'Whotcha doing?'

I jumped as though I had been caught reading something bad. Looking up I saw Hilary towering over me.

Hilary, was larger than life and not easy to be with. Games tended to grind to a halt when she turned up. Suspecting she was the cause of this, Hilary would hang around all the more, making a nuisance of herself until summoned by Enid to return indoors. Then she would slope off reluctantly, dragging the heels of her big shoes across the square.

Patty and I were playing at 'The Tree' once when Hilary had arrived. We told her we were going home for our tea but exchanged our secret sign, a brush of the hand across the forehead meaning we would return once she was safely out of the way.

'Who can I play with then?' asked Hilary. 'Mr Nobody?' It was quite sad really.

When Hilary laughed, her huge chin would fall almost down to her chest and she would emit a great bellow. She was strong and capable of things like shifting furniture as mentioned earlier, but also I suspect of other less helpful things that you couldn't quite put your finger on, theft of course being one of them.

Hilary never spoke about the special school she lived at, or her life before she became fostered by Enid. When she wasn't happy, which was probably most of the time, her face would be set in a sulky frown. But on odd occasions, like that time she took the chest of drawers upstairs for Mum and got our admiration, her face would break into a smile and her eyes become as soft as a cow's.

'Just reading,' I said in answer to her question. She sat down and picked a piece of grass to chew. The heat of the day didn't seem to bother her, dressed as she was in a pair of jeans, a roll-necked sweater and the usual heavy leather shoes.

'Monica uses those,' she said pointing to the Tampax advert with a bitten nail.

'Does she?' I asked, suddenly interested in spite of Hilary's unwanted presence. 'What for?'`

'Don't you know?'

I tried to give the impression that I was fully conversant with Tampax and its uses. Hilary saw straight through this of course and proceeded to enlighten me with regard to periods. I thought she was joking. That wouldn't be happening to me, I assured her. Mum would take me up to Doctor Mills and we'd soon get that straightened out.

Hilary gave a great spitty guffaw.

'I'd like to try that,' she said. 'I'd like him to change meh from being a girl if he could, but I doubt it.'

She always spoke like that. 'Me' was always 'meh' like upper class people spoke in old British films.

'Where's your real mum anyway?' I asked her. 'Why do you stay with Enid in the holidays?'

Hilary shrugged.

'Didn't want meh. So sent meh away.'

'Well, at least you've got Enid,' I said.

'Probably doesn't want meh either. Just puts up with meh.'

Hilary lay down and gazed at the sky like I had been doing. She seemed set for the afternoon until Alwyn sprang onto the blanket out of nowhere, her little brush of a tail going nineteen to the dozen. I was relieved when Mrs Cherry arrived soon after and suggested that Hilary might like to earn a couple of shillings by doing some digging in her back garden.

'Mr Carling's back is playing him up,' she said. 'What do you think, Hilary? Would you like to?'

'Don't mind.'

So off went Hilary leaving me in peace to mull over the question of Tampax and her laughable explanation, which I couldn't wait to repeat to Mo at the first opportunity. When Mo confirmed Hilary's story having learned all about it at Chailey, my incredulous grin froze on my face. I felt as though a huge conspiracy had been going on between all the females of the world and I was the last to know.

Across the Sea to Ireland

We went off to Ireland in the spring as Dad had promised. The rail journey was free with our passes. However, the journey to Cork was a mammoth expedition. After heading up to London by train, we took the tube to Paddington Station. The underground system fascinated me with its funny little trains shooting out of dark tunnels. Their approach built to such a crescendo that you fully expected nothing short of a dragon to emerge breathing fire.

The journey to Fishguard seemed interminable; hour after hour of being cramped in a carriage with strangers. Will and I had nothing to do except giggle about the shape of ladies hats ('Hers is like a birthday cake') or how funny people looked when they fell asleep with their mouths open ('He's got a funny little tongue in there like our Joey's').

On the excuse of going to the toilet, we'd run up and down the corridor with Anne yelling to join in. Dad was very hot under the collar and Mum was at her wit's end by the time we pulled in to Fishguard Harbour. Dad strode up the gangplank ahead of us with the suitcases. No cases on wheels in those days, just arms being pulled out of sockets. Mum carried Anne and a bag with all her immediate requirements inside, along with sandwiches and squash for the journey.

The huge bulk of the Innisfallen towered above us while people milled around the deck clutching their belongings and talking nineteen to the dozen. As we queued for our accommodation, I remember seeing a nun in front of us carrying a basket full of pigeons.

Our cabins were an improvement on our last trip when Dad had only been able to afford the reclining chairs near the deck. Mum said they were like straitjackets and she never got a wink. I remember she had bought me a blue duster coat and straw hat for that journey. She had tried several times to put the coat on me as we arrived into Cork Harbour when all I wanted to do was sleep. The hat, useless in the gale, I believe went overboard.

I had been too young to remember the trip before that, but I gather it had been even worse with no comfy chairs at all, just a wooden bench under some sort of awning. It was before Will was born and we had gone over for one of our auntie's weddings. Mo's legs had been in plaster following an operation.

On this latest trip, Will and I were in trouble before we'd even docked at Cork Harbour. We'd woken early and, finding our parents and Anne still asleep, had crept out of the cabin to explore. It was only just daylight but we could see a blur of land on the horizon. The air was damp and salty with a few seagulls shrieking along beside us. Will stood squinting at the sheer size of the sea, his hair on end like Dad's before Brylcreem. We did a bit of going up and down ladders before ending up in the galley where the cooks kindly gave us tea and toast.

When we heard our names over the tannoy we looked at each other in horror.

'I'm never bringin' ye again, ye pair o' nannygoats,' declared our dad as Mum, weak with angst, fell on the pair of us with arms outstretched. 'My Jaysis I dunno where I got ye from at all. Ye can stay with your Grandmother Wallace next time.'

However, all of this and the general pain of the journey was forgotten when Granddad and Nanny Sullivan, in her pinafore and lace up shoes, greeted us at the front door. Our Irish grandmother had the gentlest voice and the kindest ways with children having had thirteen of her own with eight surviving, Dad being the second eldest. We'd only seen her on those journeys to Cork or when she and Granddad made a rare visit to Kent. Apart from that she remained our distant 'Nanny Sullivan' who sent shamrock in a little green box every St Patrick's Day for Mum to pin on our school woollies.

'Hello, Boy,' she said hugging Dad's waist and dabbing her eyes with a hanky. Behind her, Granddad Sullivan did a sort of shout which could have been either a greeting or a telling off to us all – it was hard to know which.

'How's things over?' he asked Dad as we ate a lunch of cold ham, fluffy potatoes or 'poppies' as Nan called them and drank tea poured from a huge brown pot. 'Over' meant over the sea in England, not 'Over and Out' like on 'Whirlibirds' as Will and I joked.

Dad talked about life in Ashford, the railway works and the price of things 'over'. Granddad would answer 'My Jaysis' and 'Goway outdat' and Nan would break off from talking with Mum to answer 'Yes, Papa,' and 'No, Papa,' as though all their children were still present around the table. Granddad would often grow quite heated over a subject and bang his fist down, setting the cups rattling. This would be a cue for Will and I to slip out to the garden. We liked to play on the black railings that separated Nan Sullivan's house from the one next door. Nuala who lived there was about my own age. She was really sweet but hard to understand as she spoke in the same whispery lilt as Nanny. 'White' was 'whoite', like she was blowing a dandelion away.

Nuala's elder brother had to be kept an eye on as he was retarded. He was never allowed out for more than a few minutes at a time before his mother would call him in. Sometimes he could be seen in the back garden tottering up and down the path in his vest, hitting out at butterflies and turning around sharply to yell at imaginary presences.

All in all, there wasn't much to do at the house in Mount Carmel Road once the novelty of being there had worn off. The days would drag for us, particularly between tea time and going to bed. We found the Irish TV programmes deathly compared to those at home. Telefis Eireann hadn't much to offer in those days apart from news reports and adverts for soft drinks, crisps and ice lollies. In desperation, we often resorted to playing with the two Chinese dogs from the top of Nanny's sideboard. They were made of polished wood – one black, one brown with removable tongues. High on the wall was a three foot long alligator also in wood. It looked as though it might be a very interesting toy but understandably, was out of bounds.

After the evening meal, Granddad could often be found seated in the back yard on a dustbin, smoking a cigarette. His favourite brand were 'Majors' and we marvelled at how he could keep one in his mouth even after he'd dozed off with his back against the wall. We found him several times thus with an inch of spent ash still hanging from the filter. It was only when the cigarette burned down to his lip that he'd wake with his usual shout.

At the end of Mount Carmel Road was a huge old building that had once been a boys' college. A statue of Our Lady stood in front of it and, when viewed from outside Nanny's house, you got the impression of the long road to heaven with Our Lady at the end.

There were holy statues in Nanny's house and the homes of our aunts and uncles. In the room where our parents slept a huge picture of St Teresa hung on the wall above the bed. We slept in our Uncle Terry's room while he stayed with one of our aunts for the duration of the visit. A large wooden crucifix hung near the door and on the mantelpiece was a little white figure bearing the Sacred Heart.

To avoid having to share his single bed with me, Will was sent to Auntie Angela's on the first night of our arrival. Unfortunately, he had woken in the early hours and gone hysterical at the sight of a dark, ghostly figure on the back of the door which turned out to be nothing more than a skin diving suit. Auntie Angela had come to the fore with a hot drink but nothing would induce Will to spend another night in the 'haunted' bedroom. From then on he slept head to toe with me at Mount Carmel.

Uncle Terry, the youngest of Dad's siblings, was a handsome fellow in his youth. He would have been in his teens at the time of this particular visit. His dark good looks put one in mind of a young George Best. Handy with a bat or tennis racquet, Terry would have us out in the street hitting a ball back and forth. He'd take us for walks to 'The Lough', buying fishing nets and chocolate for us on the way. Terry used to say that the lough was a great place and so it was. The water was quite deep and Granddad said you could drown in it if you weren't careful. There was a little island where ducks and swans would congregate. It was a pretty oasis in the middle of the housing estates.

While we fished, Terry strolled off, as was his way, to walk around the edge of the lough or hang about until we'd done enough fishing. He wasn't much of a conversationalist and when he did speak his accent was so strong it was hard to follow what he was saying. We knew his heart was in the right place though, what with the chocolate and the fishing nets.

Some evenings were spent at the pub at the top of the hill. Sandwiched between our aunts and uncles, Will and I would find their laughter infectious as they recalled events from times gone by. We got swept up in the general gaiety and the novelty of seeing adults thus uninhibited. Down our club there was joy now and again but nothing like this. Most evenings culminated in a sing-song, which Mum dreaded. Dad however, would be in his element, holding forth with 'Wild Colonial Boy' and 'Star of the County Down,' his tie loosened and ears aflame as ever.

Every morning I would accompany Nanny Sullivan down the sloping old streets and across the River Lee to the English market. If we met with neighbours on the way, Nan would introduce me as the eldest of her grandchildren. Smiles were exchanged and questions asked in broad accents, sometimes even in the Irish language itself, *'Conas atá tú?'* which made answering impossible. I usually received a pat on the head or a handshake when a look of bafflement appeared on my face.

The indoor market was a chilly place with raw meat and feathers everywhere. Pigs' trotters were arranged on counters beside hams and huge mauve tongues. Fruit and vegetables were piled high and on the floor was a mix of squashed produce and bloodied sawdust. Nanny would raise her lilting voice to be heard above the din of the vendors calling out their wares. I didn't like the place any more than the butchers' shop at home, but felt privileged to be accompanying my grandmother and carrying her bag as she tapped from stall to stall in her little mousy shoes.

Like many young Irishmen, Granddad had come to England in search of work. He didn't see his family for months at a time and on his visit home the children had to be scrubbed and lined up for his inspection. In his youth Granddad had cut a fine figure according to photographs.

Granddad built a bungalow at Graball Bay, Crosshaven out of corrugated iron and raw materials from the Mercy Hospital, where he worked after returning from England. He named the place 'Ritaville' after one of my aunts who died in her early teens. The original bungalow has since been replaced by a more modern holiday home. With its view across the bay to Roches Point lighthouse, it is a wonderful place to sit and relax.

One day, Dad took us down to Crosshaven along with as many of our cousins that could be fitted into the old car he had borrowed. We were all laughing in the back as we sped along beneath the overhanging trees. On a beach of slanting, barnacled rocks we searched for baby crabs, while up the steps at the bungalow Mum and my aunts made a dinner of ham, potatoes in their jackets and huge marrowfat peas. We all dined out on the grass. Surrounded by so many of his family, Dad was in his element.

On one of our last days in Cork during that visit, Dad took us out in a boat across a flooded valley. He rowed us into the middle of the lake and showed where tree tops poked up through the water. He told us there was a church underneath whose bell still rang and stopped rowing so we could listen for it, but everything was silent apart from birdsong. Dad looked around him at the beauty of Ireland. His eyes were misty like the clouds over the mountains.

'The fields look a bit like round Sevington at home,' I said trying to share his mood.

"Tis nothing like Sevington,' replied Dad. 'This is Ireland.'

The O'Sullivan family circa 1937
(Dad in front of his father)

Dad (centre) in Cork with brothers and Jack the dog, who liked to take the bus to town (circa 1948)

Leavers

Class Four, run by Miss Smart the headmistress, was the 'Leavers' class and the last port of call before departing primary school. Here, the Eleven Plus exam would eventually be sat and our futures determined. Those successful would go to the Grammar School or the recently opened Convent, otherwise you went to one of the local secondary moderns – the North or South, depending on which side of town you lived. Class Four was much quieter than any other class as no-one dared speak unless asked to when the headmistress was in the room.

I sat at the back near the little altar next to Josephine, who had been so successful in her Christmas cracker outfit. There were books on the shelf like 'The Water Babies,' 'Ballet Shoes' and poems by Walter de la Mare. While arithmetic had become even harder, English subjects had become more interesting. We did 'dictionary' work where you were asked a question as to what a word meant. You then had to look it up and write down the answer. The first word I looked up was 'Tableau.'

'What 'T' is this?' was the question beneath a group arranged on a stage.

'I've never heard of a 'tabloo' before,' I said to Josephine.

'Well, that's the point of the exercise!' remarked the headmistress, who happened to be passing at the time.

Although she could be a 'tartar', I had a vague sort of respect for the headmistress. She was, after all, principal of the school and held great power. If she gave you any kind of praise you knew it was praise indeed, for she rarely dealt out a compliment. However, if she caught you giggling in a lesson or found you anywhere near the classroom at playtime no matter how cold the weather outside, it was 'the ruler' for you.

On Friday mornings, we listened to a classical music programme with a book for guidance. I enjoyed this, particularly when there was any ballet music involved. I was fascinated by 'Swan Lake' and 'Coppelia', the wooden doll that comes to life. Another radio programme was 'Music, Movement and Mime.' In the hall we would join in with dance and physicality which I loved.

One of our afternoon stories was 'The Silver Sword' and I would listen rapt over Ruth protecting her brother and sister as they made their way from Poland to their grandmother's house in Switzerland. Ever imaginative, I pictured myself in the same hugely responsible position, even though my brother and sisters were quite safe from the Nazis and my Nan only lived on Newtown.

Nana Spice had moved house by this time and not necessarily for the better. She had announced one afternoon while perched on the arm of our sofa that 235 was too big to keep clean and she was going to ask for a transfer to a flat. She left the house she had occupied for nearly forty years and moved into number 13 – unlucky for some, it most certainly was for her. After only a few short weeks she complained that the noisy neighbours above always had their television on loud and it was driving her 'batchy'.

When she asked me if I could hear the 'din' overhead, I wanted to say that I could not but was always in a quandary. If I said yes I could hear it, war would be waged against the Dawsons upstairs and wouldn't make for very neighbourly relations. To say I heard nothing would be letting Nan down and she'd suspect that she was in this on her own, which sadly appeared to be the case.

'Your Nan's mad,' said Tony Dawson to me in class one day. 'She keeps coming up to ours and banging on the door and going on about our telly being too loud.'

'So?' I said, shocked. 'You should turn it down then.'

'Yeah, but she comes up even when it ain't on,' he said with his goaty smile.

Looking back, I wonder if this 'noise' business wasn't the reason Nan left the old house in the first place as it wasn't very big at all by today's standards.

It would eventually be discovered that Nan was suffering from tinnitus for which there was no known cure. She didn't know this then of course as she sat outside number thirteen in the last of the daylight, too desperate to go inside. Unfortunately, she wouldn't know it until she had moved twice more in an attempt to escape the 'nuisances upstairs'.

It took a move to a top floor maisonette before she realized the noises were even closer than anticipated – in her head.

On the days when the tinnitus eased a little, Nan was good company. She had a dry sense of humour and was fun to be around. One afternoon when Mo and I were in residence at number 13 for the weekend, we were all sitting outside playing with a little 'Bingo' set from the Post Office. One of Nan's counters went missing and, after an extensive search, was eventually located in the folds of her cardigan beneath her ample bosom. This set us all roaring.

'Ooohh ack!' exclaimed Nan. 'You won't forget your old Nan, will yer?'

I don't think so.

Those overnight visits were fun when Mo came along too. This hadn't been possible of course at 235, but the little flat was accessible to her. We would be allowed to stay up and watch 'Peyton Place', even though we didn't really understand the various plots, and could read our books in bed. We'd be all tucked up with 'The Famous Five' or 'The Secret Seven' until Nan came along in her candlewick dressing gown to turn out the light. She had retired from the laundry by then and, like so many lonely people, all she wanted was a little company. The trouble was that her reserved demeanour got in the way of socialising and making friends. Therefore, having two 'giggle-arses' like us around overnight meant a great deal to her.

Winnie

Since the day of the purple bead, Winnie and I had become good friends. She lived in a big house up town. The kitchen was in the basement so there was a view of people's feet passing to and fro all the time.

Winnie's mother had a screechy voice, which travelled through the house like a badly played violin. The statues in the hallway had their heads turned under their arms as though to escape it. Mrs Clarke was tall and wore bifocals. I was on edge in her company as she always seemed to be bordering on hysteria.

'And what do you propose doing with yourselves after tea?' she asked while I helped Winnie lay the table. 'I do hope you'll go out for a walk.'

'Spec so,' answered Winnie whose laid back personality was in complete contrast to her mother's.

'Sebastian!' Mrs Clarke yelled up the stairs to her son. 'Tea time, please!'

Winnie's Dad didn't join us for tea at the table, but remained slumped behind a newspaper in the living room.

'I'm afraid it's only bread and jam,' said Mrs Clarke as we sat down.

'Oh, that's all right,' I said. 'I'm used to that.'

I didn't mean to denigrate my Mum's tea-time menu in any way. Her apple pie was the best in the world. I just meant to put the woman at her ease which was totally unnecessary of course. She leant back in her chair and laughed as though she was being tickled. I was highly embarrassed.

Sebastian, when he slid into his seat, paid no attention to anything except eating his sandwich. He wasn't very much like Winnie to look at and had the manners of a much older person. In fact, he was rather like a middle aged man in a schoolboy's clothing. He had the usual 'short back and sides' haircut with curls on the top and lots of little blonde hairs on his neck. His eyelashes were fair too and his mouth was small and round like a rosebud. This was accentuated when he chewed as he had no doubt been instructed to eat with it well and truly closed.

Sebastian mostly wore yellow jumpers and grey short trousers and lived in a world of his own, it seemed. He loved singing and would often do so at the Friday concert, choosing songs with lots of verses like 'The Happy Wanderer,' Mrs Clarke having accompanied him on the piano I'd seen in their front room. The trouble was that he'd get the words all wrong but insist on continuing so that kids began fidgeting and teachers glanced at their watches. One afternoon, as a welcome contrast, Mick got up and started on a raucous song about 'Barnacle Bill the Sailor' that he'd picked up from his elder brother who was in the army. I'm not sure that the words were the originals as he'd only sung a line or two when he was asked to sit down.

'No singing at the table, thank you, Sebastian,' said Mrs Clarke when he started tuning up.

'And what do you like best at school?' she asked turning to me.

'Bead swapping,' I said with a smile at Winnie.

'Really? That won't get you very far in life.'

I felt rather shot down in flames, as this pastime was the very foundation on which my friendship with Winnie had begun. I felt like both the pastime and I didn't match up to Mrs Clarke's standards. Looking around at the neat kitchen I compared it to our harum-scarum house. It was always noisy around our table at home and sometimes funny things would happen like Dad having gravy on his lip or the custard running out before it reached me as usual. There didn't seem much room for gaiety in the Clarke's kitchen. In fact I was quite glad when tea was over and Winnie and I could go out.

The garden next door to Winnie's was full of cats. There were eyes and tails everywhere, in bushes and under hedges. When a white-haired old lady in a mottled brown cardigan appeared in the yard banging a bucket of something indescribable, the cats gathered around mewing and rubbing themselves against her legs. She nodded and smiled when she saw us.

'Helloo, Winnie. Y' alroit?' She said, shuffling towards us in a pair of tatty slippers.

'Hello, Bridie,' said Win. 'This is my friend, Lynne.'

The old lady grasped my hand eagerly, as though she hadn't touched anyone for a long time.

'Hello, girl,' she said with her head on one side. Her smile was even wider and I saw that the few teeth she possessed were the same colours as her cardigan.

'Are ye staying over the night loike?'

'No,' I said. 'Just for tea.'

''Cos ye can come in loike and have a cuppa tea wit me. Yer mam won't mind, Win, sure she won't?'

'No, we can't, Bridie,' said Win. 'We're going up the field.'

'Ah, roite. Well next toim den, eh?'

'Mum doesn't like me to go in there,' said Win when we were a few yards from Bridie's gate. 'It smells really bad, like pee. She's got loads of money, though and she's really kind. She gave me a half crown once out of a tin and told me to keep it under my hat.'

'Under your hat?'

'She meant don't tell my Mum. I'd have to give it back if she knew.'

'What did you spend it on?' I asked.

'I went down the town and got one of those diaries with a key in it you can lock up.'

'What colour did you get?' I asked, having seen these diaries in Woolworths in pink, blue and white with a little gold lock on the side.

'Pink,' said Winnie. 'I keep it under my bed and I write in it every night.'

Winnie was smiling as though she was proud to have this secret from her mother. She had a funny, stretched little smile like her mouth was too small to accommodate it. When Winnie found something really funny, she'd laugh till her face turned red and tears came.

Up at the field we talked about being in Class Four and the people we liked and those we did not and where we thought we might go if we passed our Eleven Plus. We didn't fancy the North or the South and we decided the grammar school girls looked snooty and rather posh.

'I'll be going to the Convent if I pass,' said Winnie. 'Mum says.'

I hoped I would too, but we didn't know what the exam entailed. I knew I would do well in English but if any difficult arithmetic was involved I knew it would be the North for me.

'My Dad's going to take you home in the car,' said Winnie when it was time to leave.

'Thank you for having me,' I said from the kitchen door. Mrs Clarke was still seated at the table smoking a cigarette and reading the paper. She turned and looked at me through her round glasses. 'Oh, goodbye,' she said as though she had forgotten I was ever there.

Winnie's Dad's car smelled of old leather and cigarettes. He drove it the same way he'd been reading his newspaper in their front room – slumped down in the seat. Sitting beside him, Winnie turned to smile at me like she knew her Dad was a bit strange but that he was OK really. I believed her even though I never heard him speak a word.

Mass on Sunday

On Monday mornings, the headmistress would interrogate us about who had and who had not been to Mass the previous day. It was like the TV licence detector van; if you had attended you never got quizzed but if you had not, she homed in on you like radar. If we hadn't managed to get up to the ten o'clock at St Teresa's in the morning, Dad would drive Will and I to the six o'clock at St Simon's. He did his best to keep this up but as time went on attendances fell off due to a mixture of his increasing workload and our bad behaviour when we did actually make it to the service.

The old St Teresa's church, where our parents had been married and where we had all been christened, was charming. Unfortunately, as with many of Ashford's lovely buildings, it has since been knocked down and replaced by something modern and less inspiring. The old church had been dark and atmospheric with dramatic 'Stations of the Cross' along each wall. The sun angling across the pews through beautiful stained glass windows would light up its interior. There was always a comforting light in the form of a little red lantern hanging from the ceiling. On Feast Days like Ash Wednesday when we were bussed up from school, incense burned and wreathed up to the rafters so that you felt you really were in a holy place. The confessional box was tucked away in a corner near a narrow little staircase that led up to the organ loft. It was up here that Will and I preferred to sit in order to get a good view of the congregation below.

The reason for our bad behaviour was due to boredom and being too young really to take in the importance of the Mass. Had we been raised in Ireland, where life seemed to revolve around the Church, this would have been a different matter. We received some form of religious instruction daily at school, so had grasped the basic principle of being good and doing unto others. However, we always found something amusing during the service and unfortunately the hushed atmosphere, along with the knowledge that the worst thing you could do was giggle in that holy place, only made us worse.

One Sunday, our ticklish mood was building towards hysteria when the priest, who that day was Father Ambrose, got to the reading out of 'special intentions'. We'd been rattling them off verbatim in the car on the way there. 'Mrs O'Flaherty, Mr Cruickshank, Mrs O'Grady, Terry O'Donahue' and chuckling over what on earth these intentions could be as these same people had had them for years and obviously still not got what they wanted.

The reading out of these names was even more hilarious as it coincided with the collection basket being handed along our row of seats. We had to disturb Dad, who'd adopted his usual position for worship, down on one knee with a hand across his eyes, for a couple of pennies. He fished in his pocket and produced the coins by which time the basket and its bearer were half way down the stairs.

Will leaned over the banister and dropped the coins down much to the surprise of the basket bearer, an old round shouldered fellow who sometimes helped out at the altar. He glanced up in surprise at the arrival of these 'Pennies from Heaven.' Needless to say, Will and I were both helpless and sat shaking and gasping for breath during the remainder of the service.

'My Jaysis, that's the last time I'm taking ye to Mass, ye pair of bastard nuisances,' said Dad on the way back to the lorry. 'Ye should be ashamed of yeselves, ye heathens, ye.'

'Oh, duck!' sympathised Mum at the lunch table. 'You know what they're like. I dunno why you bother.'

Dad mopped his chin of gravy and blinked his eyes in hurt indignation.

'Tell Father why you don't go to Mass.'

The headmistress was talking to Patrick the next morning as Father Joe looked on.

'I haven't got any nice clothes to wear,' murmured Patrick who was seated across from me at the back of the classroom.

'Sure, those clothes you are wearing are very nice,' said Father Joe, unaware that this was Patrick's daily attire, schooldays and weekends alike.

'I've never got any money for the bus fare,' said Patrick.

'Our blessed Lord had no money and walked all over the Holy Land,' said Father Joe. 'Surely you can walk a couple of miles to church?'

This was a valid point. Hadn't we seen Patrick, grey towel in hand, walking up to the swimming baths several times during the summer? The church wasn't that much further on so Patrick could have made it if he'd really wanted to, I decided preening myself over attending the previous day despite having behaved appallingly.

'You should always go to Mass and thank God for everything you have,' said Father Joe.

Patrick just merely smiled his broken fence smile and gazed wistfully at his bitten down finger nails. Patrick, who scrounged pennies for chips, who was never in the dinner queue on those chilly days when we lined up for a 'big one', had nothing to say.

Hello and Goodbye

'Your mum's gonna have her hands full,' remarked one of the neighbours gathered beside Mr Bickle's bread van. It was now common knowledge around the square that there was to be a new addition to our family. 'When's it due?'

'Has she thought of any names yet?' asked another. 'And is she having it in hospital or at home?'

Mum didn't usually bother with Mr Bickle's wares but had given the last of the bread to Dad that morning for his sandwich of cheese and pickle. She said she could have sworn there was another loaf in the cupboard and she didn't know whether she was coming or going these days and it wasn't surprising what with 'everything'.

'April,' I answered to the first question and 'Catherine if it's a girl,' to the second. 'We don't know about a boy's name yet.'

Further interrogations took place as to 'hospital' or 'home' and whether Dad would be disappointed if it wasn't a boy with three girls already. Having no further answers I reverted to my usual ploy of concentrating on something else instead. In this case, it was the van's handle which seemed to me to resemble a tiny boxing glove or a monkey's fist. Mr Bickle's spine was bent from years of tugging the van, which, when operated, hummed like a giant bee around the streets with the aid of this handle. Mr Bickle wore his money bag across him like a school satchel. He bent his knees each time he tipped it up to get change out, leaning so far backwards you'd think he might topple over. It was difficult to make out what Mr Bickle said, as his mouth was secreted behind the overhang of a moustache resembling a miniature yard brush but I made out 'Noinpence' and 'Thanking yew'.

I could see an array of delicious looking cakes inside the van but remembered Mum's comment about it being a 'short' week which meant no overtime for Dad and not to get ideas. Therefore, a coconut sponge with a cherry on top had to remain where it was.

'Why don't you make some lemon tops if you want cake?' suggested Mum when I grumbled. 'And don't forget the egg this time.'

That had been a silly oversight on my last baking attempt, I had to admit. My Victoria Sandwich had looked like a couple of drain covers stuck together. Nowadays think 'frisbee'.

I'd read somewhere that baby's grew from eggs, so why wasn't there a chick in every one I wondered as I beat a yolk into the mix? I had asked this of Simone at school, who then tried to tell me where babies came from. I'd laughed my head off. I'd never heard such a load of rubbish in my life and I told her so.

'But it's true,' she said. 'My Mum and Dad do it all the time and so do yours. They must do!'

I wouldn't have been surprised at her parents doing such a thing but to imply that mine did and on a regular basis was really the end.

'No, it's eggs,' I said.

'Yes, but not just eggs on their own,' laughed Simone. 'They have to be fertilised for goodness sake. Honestly, you really are backward!'

I had resented this remark. How could I be backward? I was top of the class for spelling and I knew all about looking after babies and making bottles and cooking 'Welsh Rarebit'. I decided it was because Simone often went up town and hung around with older girls that she got those funny ideas. Eggs were responsible, and that's all there was to it.

The 'egg product' arrived through a hole near Mum's belly button, as far as I was concerned, in the early hours of an April morning. I woke to the sound of a little voice crying and, shortly afterwards, Mum and Nan choosing from a box of Milk Tray. In the distance, train wagons clattered as though gossiping at the news. Next day, when I met Catherine for the first time, my parent's bedroom smelled of baby and milk and brand new life. My mother, relieved and rosy, went off for a bath leaving me with my new sister. It seems trite to say that Catherine had a face like a little peach, but there is no other way to describe it. Her cheeks were covered in a silky down which I couldn't stop touching through the slats of the cot where she lay, occupying very little space.

Catherine had been named after our Nanny Sullivan and, although he had hoped for a boy, Dad was delighted with her. He could quieten her crying in an instant and often ate his meals holding her in the crook of his arm.

Another amazing and extremely surprising event soon after this was the passing of my 'Eleven Plus.' My parents were delighted and plans were made for me to attend the Convent school along with Winnie and Simone, who had also been successful. My uniform was ordered from Lewis and Hylands. Everything was bought a size bigger to allow for growth, including my hat for some reason, so it must have been assumed that I would do very well! Sandals had been specified on the list, the crepe-soled buckle type which were clumsy and outdated. Having begun to develop airs and graces, it wasn't long before I dumped these and demanded a more dainty variety which, luckily, Mr Armstrong was able to supply after shinning up his ladder.

My last day at primary school whizzed by. I vaguely remember having my name called out with all of those who were leaving and taking my shoe bag off its peg. A new young life had begun at home and my own life was going to start changing quite drastically in the coming September. But with the six week summer holiday about to begin what did I care! I ran on ahead of Will and Mick, past the waving trees, out of the school gate and across the road for home, Mr Smedley's car only missing me by inches.

With These Hands, a memoir by the author's sister, Maureen Fenner is available for £10.00 from mofenner@fsmail.net